'Tuy An

A Year of Trying to Help

By

Richard Carl Wieburg

ISBN-10: 1479276189
EAN-13: 9781479276189
Library of Congress Control Number: 2012920861
CreateSpace Independent Publishing Platform
North Charleston, South Carolina

DEDICATION:

To my best friend, my partner, and the love of my life, Joeline,
and
To my two fantastic children, Jody and Tomey.
"Y'all" are the best team I ever "coached".
Thanks for all of your love and support through the years.

CONTENTS

My wife and I visited my loving mother, Billie Jean Wieburg, in
Arkansas just before I left for my tour of duty in Viet Nam. She
insisted that I have this picture taken in my "Dress Uniform" before I
left. She was extremely proud of me, but was obviously very concerned
about my safety, and I know she prayed for me every day that I was
in the war zone. Unfortunately, she was the one who did not make it
through that long year that I was in Nam.

Chapter 1

DYING FOR A CAUSE

Viet Nam, 1968-1969

As I studied the lush, green valley below us, I started to lose touch with the present. My mind wandered from the hillside where we had stopped and I involuntarily, or perhaps intentionally, began to drift away from my immediate situation and the ugly reality that was about to force itself onto my present. Of course that is a very dangerous thing to do when one is in the middle of a war, but sometimes the mind goes on automatic and tries its best to keep sanity in perspective.

I temporarily forgot the time, the heat, and the bugs as I gazed over the beautiful Vietnamese landscape. The dark green of the trees and thick dark foliage gave way to the lighter green of the grass around a plot of land that a farmer was plowing below the hill on which I sat. The farmer didn't seem to be afraid of, or worrying about anything, so why should I? He just trudged lazily along in the wake of his water buffalo, and I could see steam coming off both man and animal from the brief shower that had just soaked all of us. His furrows were straight and true. He was obviously an old hand at his task and knew what he was doing. He was probably plowing the same plot of ground his forefathers had plowed thousands of years before him. Or, were they his forefathers? Maybe it was the same man, living on and on in some sort of suspended time warp that had descended upon his fields, and his country.

The idea was at first absurd, but the more I thought about it, the more plausible it became. The methods of farming had undergone no

1

revision in all of those years; the land had certainly not changed; the animals were the same as those used in Egyptian times; so what of the man himself? Why couldn't he be the same individual who had plowed that same field a thousand years ago?

The District Chief, Dai Uy Be, let out a yell and I was brought sharply back to reality. Be had pulled one of his pistols and was angrily waving everyone away from the prisoners. From what I could gather in a matter of seconds, one of the prisoners, the one that I had been sure was a VCI, (Viet Cong Infrastructure) had spit in Be's face in answer to one of Be's questions.

What would have prompted the man to do such a thing was beyond me. Everyone in the District, including the Viet Cong, knew that Be was half crazy, and no one in his right mind would ever intentionally do anything to provoke him. This prisoner had just made the biggest mistake of his life.

I glanced at Be. The spittle was running down his cheek, but that was not what attracted my attention, nor was it the pistol he was waving. What always caught my attention at times like these were Be's eyes. Usually they were calm and placid, but when he went into one of these fits of rage, they became the eyes of a madman. The pupils expanded and seemed to almost emit a glow. I swear, if he had been in a dark room, you could read by them. In my year in Viet Nam I saw this happen several times and I will never forget each incident. Whatever the reason, the cause, or the physical metamorphosis that occurred in Be's eyes when he became enraged, they always struck an almost paralytic terror in anyone who was unlucky enough to be the focus of their gaze.

I knew that if I didn't immediately intervene, the prisoner had sealed his own fate. He hadn't had much of a chance of surviving from the second we captured him, but now he had none. He had to have recognized Be. He had to have known that he was already in very deep trouble, and then, to spit on Be? All I can figure, even after all of the intervening years, is that the man must have, like Be, gone temporarily insane. Somewhere during the course of answering Be's questions, the guy must have finally just flipped out and said, "the hell with this", and decided he didn't want to live anymore.

If I couldn't snap Be out of his temporary insanity, the man was certainly going to get his wish.

An hour earlier I had asked Be if I could send in the POW report on the two men. The report was nothing more than a radio message to Province alerting them to the fact that we had two prisoners, their physical condition and my opinion as to their rank and position as VCI, or whether they were simply VC. If I sent the report then Be would have to be very careful with his interrogation techniques, and both men would have to be sent to Tuy Hoa, and then on to Saigon, within 48 hours - alive. The shake of Be's head had told me all I needed to know about the chances of survival for these two men.

I could have sent the report without his approval, and most people reading this will say that I was required to do so - humanely speaking. Of course, if I had done so, one of two things would have happened; I would have been shot by Be, which would mean that Barnes, my 18 year old radio operator, would also have to be killed so that there would be no American witnesses; or Be would have had me transferred out of his District. I had once asked my controller in Tuy Hoa, a civilian named Mr. Clarkson, about disobeying Be when it came to a situation like this and he gave me strict orders that I do whatever I had to do to keep myself in this District. Clarkson said that a good working relationship between the District Chief and me was of prime importance to the success of the PHOENIX program in Phu Yen Province and that "a greater good" would be achieved by my putting any moral and/or political opinions aside to make sure that relationship continued.

As for you, the reader, right now I only ask that you finish this book before you make a final judgment in regard to Be and especially in regard to my actions, or lack thereof.

Barnes scrambled away from the prisoners, but as he had only been in country for a short while, he really had no idea what was about to happen. I yelled at Be to calm down, but he was too enraged to listen.

3

I tried to cover the yards separating us, but Barnes had inadvertently scooted between us and I had to quickly try to get around him. Be wasted no more words. He had grabbed the prisoner by the hair and drug the poor guy a few feet away from the second man. Then he simply placed one of his pearl handled 45's next to the man's forehead and as I yelled again, he pulled the trigger. My second shout was lost in the thunder of the pistol.

As I yelled, I glanced away from Be and was staring directly at the prisoner when the gun went off. In that split second I saw that he was not screaming for mercy, nor was he wildly looking around for help. He was simply staring straight ahead with a relatively calm expression on his face. He knew what was coming and he had accepted it. Whatever his faith, he had embraced it and was calmly accepting his fate.

I stopped in mid stride and glanced over to watch Barnes' reactions: at least that was what I told myself. He was staring, not believing what he was witnessing. He jumped a little on the second and third shots, then he also turned his head away, towards me, as Be emptied the remainder of the cylinder through what was left of the man's head. Our eyes locked and held.

I had seen the result of the first bullet and didn't want to see the result of the other five, but even that would have been better than trying to answer the questions that sprang to Barnes' eyes. I did not have the answers, nor did I care to search my soul for them.

Actually what I thought was, "*Damn, why did I have him carry my radio today? Why didn't I have Corporal Clack or Sgt. Thomas? They both had been in the country for months and knew the score. Neither of them would question me with their stares. They would turn away and pretend not to see anything. They would never talk about what had happened and they certainly would not question me in regard to the incident. Barnes' eyes told me he was going to have a lot of questions.*"

I glanced back to the peaceful valley searching for the ageless farmer and the tranquility that surrounded him, but he was gone. The sky was still blue, the green of the jungle was still beautiful, the water buffalo still stood in the middle of a furrow with the wooden plow still attached, but the farmer had disappeared. So, he was afraid of something after all. Maybe he was a mere mortal like the rest of us.

While I searched the splendid landscape, looking for the farmer and trying to again forget the present, a few incidental things kept registering in the back of my mind. I could hear someone throwing up and knew it had to be Barnes. I could hear the second prisoner crying and mumbling incoherently, and I could hear Dai Uy Be's calm, tranquil voice almost instilling sanity to an insane scene.

I remember thinking, *"What a beautiful country this is,"* and then hearing Be calling me. The second prisoner, it seemed, had decided he wanted to talk. Through bouts of sobbing and blowing his nose, he pointed to another hill about a mile away, and described a cave which he said was the hiding place of the VC (Viet Cong) group for which we had been searching.

Be told me we would move out immediately to attack the hill. I interrupted him abruptly, and told him in no uncertain terms that now he was going to listen to me. I was there to give military advice and he was going to listen. I told him I would radio the Air Force Base in Tuy Hoa and see if I could get us an airstrike. I reminded him that there was a pretty good sized group of VC on that hill and that they certainly had that cave fortified. I told him we would definitely lose some men if we attacked it by charging the hill and with the modern technology we had available to us, those would be senseless casualties. I also told him that if an air strike was not possible, then I would call the Army and check on the chance of an artillery bombardment. Charging a hill like we were with Roosevelt's Rough Riders was the last thing on my military advice check list. If there was a way to get this job done without unduly risking lives, mine included, then I was going to find it.

The sanity returned to Be's eyes and he agreed to wait to see what I could come up with.

I plotted the coordinates on my map and gave Barnes the task of calling the Air Base and requesting an air strike on the cave the prisoner had, to save his own life, identified for us. I figured Barnes needed some activity to get his mind at least partially off of what he had just witnessed.

By then, most of the Vietnamese troops that had accompanied us had spread out around the hill we were on and were devouring the balls of rice they carried in their packs. They totally ignored the dead man lying near us and went about eating their lunch. A single life meant very little to them. Most of them had been fighting their entire lives and had long ago lost any compassion for those they considered their enemies.

I took off my helmet and wiped the sweat from the inside liner with a sweat rag I always carried. I checked for the tenth time to make sure my M-16 safety was on, and then walked a few yards up the hill where I could look back to make sure my PRU (my mercenary squad members) were interspersed with the regular Vietnamese soldiers around the perimeter.

These actions were useless and unnecessary. The PRU had been doing this for years, and surviving. They didn't need me to tell them how to protect a perimeter. In truth, I was partially trying to get my mind off of what had just happened, but mainly I was trying to keep from having to talk to Barnes.

I again tried to lose myself in the beautiful scenery, but the remaining prisoner kept pulling me back to reality with his continued sobbing. I understood that he was afraid for his life, and was probably traumatized by the death of his companion, but I knew the noise he was making was going to eventually aggravate Be. His sobbing was definitely not increasing his chances for survival.

Finally, I called my interpreter, Gem, over and asked him to find out why the man was still crying and try to shut him up before Be shot him.

"Dai Uy's not going to kill him, is he?" I asked. "I cannot allow that!" I added.

"No, he will be free to go after the jets arrive."

"Then find out why he is still crying and shut him up. Maybe the dead guy was his brother or something."

Barnes told me that we had our jets, but I would have to communicate directly with the pilots when they arrived.

Gem went over to the guy and began talking. He calmed him down enough that they could have a broken, halting conversation. A few minutes later he returned to where I was seated, knelt down beside me, and pulled up a blade of grass to chew on. He didn't say anything for a few minutes and it was obvious he was forming the correct English words. I could still hear the other guy sobbing. I waited.

Finally he muttered, in a voice a lot softer than I had heard him use before, "His wife, son, and mother are in that cave."

I stared at Gem. I was completely stunned. I held my breath as I tried to take in what he had told me. The only thing I could think to do was seek confirmation. "Are you telling me that this guy just told us where his wife and kid - and mother are, so we can kill all of them instead of him.?" Gem simply nodded.

I had just learned a quick and very unpleasant lesson in human nature: When faced with certain death, a man will often do or say anything, or take any gamble, to try to prolong his own life.

I like to think that this man would have given his life for his family if there had been no question as to whether they would die if he talked. I have always rationalized his problem, as I'm sure he did in those few seconds when he had to decide what to do. He must have felt that there was a good chance his family would not actually be in the cave at that moment. After all, they didn't spend 24 hours a day there. They used the cave mostly at night as shelter and protection. There was a good chance they would be out seeking food or whatever, and there was also a good chance that they wouldn't be killed even if they were unlucky enough to be there when the Vietnamese forces arrived. So, he gambled.

Unfortunately for him and his family, I called in an airstrike, and there simply is no negotiating with Napalm and High Explosives. The guy lost his gamble!

The jet roared in from the west and I had Barnes throw a smoke grenade to identify our position I didn't want that jet making any mistakes. Then I confirmed the suspected location of the VC and told the pilot where on the hill I felt the cave would be.

Many things in this world are both pretty, and deadly; a coral snake, a panther, and even a woman, but nothing is any prettier and at the same time more deadly than Napalm. Its bright orange flames contrasted sharply with the green foliage it consumed in the jungles of Viet Nam, and it was certainly deadly. Burning at about 2000 degrees, it cinderizes anything with which it came into contact. It flowed like lava into foxholes, bunkers, trenches, ditches, and caves. It stuck to anything it touched, including human skin, and once on the skin, there was virtually no realistic way of getting it off. Even if a person was lucky enough not to be actually touched by it, the Napalm could still kill with hyperthermia, radiant heat, dehydration, suffocation, smoke inhalation, and carbon monoxide poisoning.

In terms of area, one firebomb released from a low-flying plane can damage an area of 2,500 square yards. Thus, I made very certain that we were not even close to the suspected location of the cave.

The jet dropped Napalm to clear the area, and then a little later came back with HE (High Explosives) in case the cave needed to be penetrated.

It was going to take us quite some time to reach the impact area, and we needed the time to let the area cool. We had to get back down off of the hill we were on, walk along the edge of the field where the farmer had been plowing, circle another hill, and then climb through the jungle that covered the hill where he told us the cave was. We also had to be very careful in case the man had sent us into an elaborate ambush.

Once we got half way up the hill, we had no trouble finding what we were looking for. It had probably just been a depressed area in the hill, with a rock overhang and not a real cave at all, but it was hard to tell too much what it would have looked like before the jet arrived. We found a total of what was probably about 13 bodies, or parts of bodies, strewn about the area in various orders of disarray, most of the tissues having been burned away by the Napalm. We found many weapons and parts of weapons indicating that this place was a well-armed camp. Somehow, that fact still does not comfort me much when I am forced to recall the incident.

Two days later we learned that the second prisoner, whom Be had released after we left the area, had been murdered, or killed, or assassinated, whatever you want to call it, by the VC for exposing his comrades. His mother and wife had been killed in the cave. His son had not been there and had survived, but he was forced to live with the knowledge that his own father had caused the deaths of his family members.

At this point you are going to start second guessing my actions, and I am sure you have already formed your opinion of Be. It is only natural that you do so. But, let me give you some specific questions to ponder.

If I had not called for jets, and if the women and children had stayed out of the firefight that would have occurred when we arrived at the cave, they probably would have survived and would have been released later that day. But, if we had attacked the cave on foot, without the jets, there is no doubt that some of my men would have been killed in the battle. So, militarily I did the right thing.

But morally? By calling the jets I killed quite a few "innocent" civilians.

Be's terrible elimination of the prisoner got us the information we needed, and doubtless saved us many lives as this band of VC had already killed many people - that's why we were looking for them in the first place.

So, in war, does the end justify the means?

Was there justice in the second prisoner's being assassinated by his own people?

Questions and second guessing will drive a soldier insane. That's why, in this book, I will try not to moralize or excuse the actions in which I was involved. It would be useless for me to do so. I did not have the answers 45 years ago, and even though I am older, and hopefully "wiser", I still do not have them.

However, the contrast between that beautiful valley and the horrible deaths that were dealt out that day still intrigues me. What is worth dying for? Isn't an honorable death, a death just the same? Was that prisoner, who a few days later died dishonorably, any better off, or worse off, than the one Be killed? There is a poem by Phil George that I used to teach in my English classes.

9

They said, "You are no longer a lad."
I nodded.
They said, "Enter the council lodge."
I sat.
They said, "Our lands are at stake."
I scowled.
They said, "We are at war."
I hated.
They said, "Prepare red war symbols."
I painted.
They said, "Count coups."
I scalped.
They said, "You'll see friends die."
I cringed.
They said, "Desperate warriors fight best."
I charged.
They said, "Some will be wounded."
I bled.
They said, "To die is glorious"
They lied.

I am an old English teacher, basketball coach, and school administrator. I am certainly not a philosopher. But, what I have come to realize, and what I believe, is that to a man, how he lives is what's important, not how he dies. The manner of death is important only to his friends, relatives, and enemies. To a man who is right with God, and right with himself, the living makes all the difference. The Living is what is Glorious, not the Dying.

But, I am getting way ahead of myself. We need to go back to the beginning of this story so that you can see where I am coming from, and see how I got to this beautiful hill in South Viet Nam.

Chapter 2
LETTER FROM UNCLE SAM

When I started college at Arizona State University I was completely broke. My father borrowed money from the man he was training horses for at that time, Mr. Charles Mickle, to pay my initial tuition. However, it would be up to me to pay that money back, as well as to pay for my own room and board, and anything else I would need to continue in college past that first semester. I was on my own.

I was able to do this by taking classes until noon, working for Sears in the Customer Service Department from 1 pm until 9 pm, and then babysitting brood mares at Mr. Mickle's ranch from 10 pm until 7am.

The job at Sears was great, because after about 5:00pm, hardly anyone came to customer service. All I had to do was sit at the counter and work on my college homework. When anyone came to the department with a broken toaster or whatever, I helped them, and when they left, I went back to my homework. I will always have a soft spot in my heart for Sears because of the way they treated me during those five years.

Mr. Mickle paid me the same $1.25 an hour that I was making at Sears to sleep in the mare barn during foaling season and take care of the mares who were foaling. It was an easy job. I could do homework, sleep, and eat in the barn. The mare barn was more modern and certainly cleaner than the apartment in which I was living. I quickly learned what to look for in regard to when the mares were actually going to foal and most nights after I finished my homework, I could just go to sleep. Of course I had to get up every 30 or 45 minutes to check the mare's progress, so I learned to go to sleep immediately and wake up the same way.

If a mare happened to foal while I was there, I simply watched to make sure there were no complications. When the foal came out, I tore the sack off, made sure the nose was clear, gave a penicillin shot, and enjoyed the first hour or so of life for the new foal. If there were complications, I called Mr. Mickle's grown son, Wes, who ran the ranch. He would come down and make the decision as to whether or not we should call the vet. It was a great job. At 7:00am, I left for my 7:40 college class.

However, by the time my junior year rolled around, I was getting married and was going to need more money. The ROTC classes I had taken the first two years were required of every male student, and of course they did not pay us to take them. But, if I signed up for ROTC classes my junior year, the Army would pay me $40 a month. Of course this meant that I was committing to a minimum of two years in the Army after I graduated, but the money was too good to pass up. Besides, I liked the military history and military tactics classes and had no problem with going into the Army as a Second Lieutenant after graduation.

Once I was married, things got a lot easier for me. My wife, Joeline, got a job at the Sears store in downtown Phoenix so we didn't see each other during the day. But, she loved horses, so at night she went with me to Mickle's mare barn. We thoroughly enjoyed having that time together. We cooked pizzas in the sterilization oven that was used by the vet, played cards, and she helped me with my homework. Sleep? We were kids and newly married, we didn't need sleep.

When I finally did graduate, after five years at Arizona State, I was sent to Fort Benning, Georgia for Infantry training. We left for Benning with no money, but with a Chevron credit card. We used it to pay for gas, and Howard Johnson Hotels accepted it as payment for rooms. Therefore, we stayed at those hotels, charged our meals to our rooms and arrived at Benning in fine style, but with absolutely no cash.

The first thing I did was to go to the pay master and ask for my pay. I was quickly informed that I would get pay at the end of the month like everyone else. I realized we were in trouble. It was the 4th of June and we had no apartment, no food, and no money. So, I asked where I could borrow money. I was sent to another office and was given a small amount of cash that had to be paid back out of my first paycheck. It was not enough to rent an apartment, so we started looking and found a room that could be rented in an old house. As it turned out the lady who owned the house was certifiably insane and carried a shotgun with her at all times. We had no choice and rented the room.

Everything worked out. I loved Fort Benning and the Army. I got to play war games, do a lot of physical conditioning, and sit in on military training classes that were very similar to the ones I had taken in college. The physical conditioning had never been a problem for me. In fact, I was the only cadet at Arizona State who scored a perfect 500 points on the Physical Training exercises during the required military summer camp in Fort Lewis, Washington, which was held between our junior and senior years in college. I think that is why I was named "Distinguished Military Student" and "Distinguished Military Graduate". It was certainly not because of my grade point average.

Of course, we spent quite a few nights out in the woods around Fort Benning practicing escape and evasion, search and destroy, and other military maneuvers that the Army felt we would need in the future. I was having a great time, and getting paid for it.

However, it had become very clear that most of our futures would center on Viet Nam. We began to realize that very soon we would have to leave our wives and families for at least a year and go there. Of course we had known that this was a possibility from the time we signed up at the beginning of our junior years, but most of us kept thinking that the war would be over long before the Army had us trained enough to be given a company of men and send into battle.

Joeline, got to spend the days at the Fort Benning Officers' Club with its two swimming pools. She had worked and/or gone to school every day of her life up until then, so this was a very nice vacation for her. The only real problem was that we were flat broke. If it hadn't been for the lack of money it would have been perfect.

After a couple of months of this training, I was sent to Fort Hood, Texas where I was supposed to be an armored platoon leader. The Infantry was using APC's (Armored Personnel Carriers), and I was supposed to be a platoon leader in charge of a group of men and their APC's. However, when I arrived, the first thing I saw tacked up on a bulletin board was an announcement about basketball tryouts for the Battalion team, and the need of a coach.

I had played basketball all through high school, and although I was not very good, I loved the game and had become a student of it. In college I took as many basketball coaching classes as I could. I played Varsity Tennis my freshman year at ASU, but was certainly not good enough to even try out for the Varsity Basketball team, but I became friends with the Varsity coach and learned a great deal from him. So, although I had no coaching experience, I immediately got an interview with the Battalion Commander and managed to convince him that I was the next "Bobby Knight" of basketball coaching and he gave me the job of being the Battalion basketball coach.

Again, it was a great assignment for me. I was a player coach, so I got to play and coach the game I loved and at the same time avoid the boring training that the other new Lieutenants were going through on the extremely hot plains around Ft. Hood. I was lucky enough to have some tremendous players come out for the team. One was an All American from West Virginia and one was a street kid from Philly who had never been to college but was a natural talent. I quickly learned that I was not in their league as a player and so I quit playing and just concentrated on coaching.

I am not being modest when I say that I started out not knowing what I was doing. Again, I had played some high school basketball but even as a senior I was not even a starter on the small high school team. But, I was smart enough to listen and definitely not too proud to get help. The guy from West Virginia spent time alone with me on the court teaching me an offense he thought we could use, and then I taught it to the whole team. The private from Philadelphia taught me the press he and his buddies used to destroy other teams on the playgrounds there,

14

and I quickly adopted it. In fact, I continued to use it for over 30 of coaching in the states after I got out of the Army.

We ended up going all the way to the Post Championship game and that season cemented my will be a basketball coach once my Army career was over.

The only negative thing that happened to Joeline and I while we were at Fort Hood was that shortly after the basketball season was over, the Lieutenant from West Virginia (I am not using his name on purpose) was driving his new Jaguar at over 100 miles an hour and rolled it. He was killed instantly. He was a wonderful young man with all the potential in the world. His death was a terrible shock to all of us.

At about that same time, most of the guys began to get orders that they were being sent to Viet Nam. A few did get a reprieve and were sent to posts in Germany and one guy actually got orders for Hawaii, but for the majority, Viet Nam was in their immediate future. I knew that I would probably be going, and once the season was over and we had a little time, the uncertainty had begun to wear thin on both Joeline and me.

When I did receive my orders in April, they were, as expected, for Nam. I was to have a thirty day leave, then I would be sent to Panama for Jungle School, then to Viet Nam as a platoon leader for the 4th Infantry Division. I did some checking and found that the life expectancy for a new Second Lieutenant with the 4th was less than a month. My father had trained race horses all his life and I had grown up with gambling, odds, and statistics as a way of life. Those were certainly not good odds, but, then again, I always did like longshots.

My father had not gone past the 6th grade in school, and my mother had only graduated from the 8th. Although I always felt that they were very intelligent people regardless of their lack of education, what were the odds that their son would graduate from a major university? I had played tennis for only two years at a small high school. What were the odds that I would end up a Varsity Letterman at a major university? Odds mean nothing. It is what you actually do that counts.

We spent some of the 30 day leave in Arkansas where my mother and father were living and then went to California where Joeline's mom lived. The thirty days flew by and all of a sudden there was no more time.

Was I interested in going to a war in a place called Viet Nam? There was no way that I wanted to go. But, that was what I signed up for by taking the Army's money during my ROTC days and now it was time to pay up.

Was I afraid that I would be killed? No, I can't say that I was. It wasn't that I thought I was special and I was certainly not a hero and looking for glory. I was simply young and felt that I was invincible. OK, you are right! Maybe a better way to put it would be to say, "I was young and stupid". Sure, I knew that many young lieutenants were getting killed over there, but that was them, not me!

When you were young, did you drive your car or motorcycle too fast? You knew the odds of accidents, but accidents happen to the other drivers, not you. Right? I guess I had the same mentality.

One of my best friends, Hank Rhodes, a guy I had gone through ROTC with, and who had driven to California for my wedding a couple of years before, called from Phoenix. He asked if it would be all right if he drove over the day I was to leave to see me off. He actually did drive all the way from Phoenix to Fresno so that he could be there when I left and would be there for my wife, Joeline, to give her a shoulder to cry on, if she needed it. Someone who is willing to drive over 13 hours one way, just to see his buddy get on a plane is a real friend, and I will never forget the kindness Hank showed us. True friends are hard to find. As far as the Army went, Hank had been one of the lucky ones, as his orders were for an honor guard unit in Virginia.

When the plane took off from Fresno I was glad of one thing - that the countdown of days had finally started. The only way to get the year over so that I could return to my life with Joeline was to have the year of war begin.

I had made out a will, visited with my relatives, said my goodbyes, and was as ready as I was ever going to be to go to war. I was a 24 year old Lieutenant in the United States Infantry and although I would have rather stayed in America, I was proud of the fact that I would be serving my country. Unfortunately, many of my countrymen did not agree with my feelings.

A year and what seemed like many lifetimes later, when I left Viet Nam for the last time, my feelings were basically the same. I was an average American soldier. I did not return as a drug addict. I did not return as a raving lunatic. I did not return as a war hero. I simply returned after having served my year. There were no bands to welcome me home, but neither was I spit on or called names. Most people simply did not want to talk to me about my experiences and would rather just ignore the fact that I had been to Nam.

The flashbacks that torment so many Viet Nam veterans seldom bother me. I can speak openly about what I saw and did, and although I made mistakes, I am not going to try to make excuses or apologize for them. I do not believe that the mistakes I made were intentional, with evil intent, or premeditated. I simply made mistakes.

War is horrible. It is not, as the Rambo movies portray it, glamorous, heroic, and exciting. Those movies are great entertainment and I enjoy them, but, they are not real life. They do not show war, or Viet Nam as it really was.

The North Vietnamese and Viet Cong soldiers were not stupid and cowards. Many of them believed in their cause as fervently as I believed in mine and were prepared to die for their beliefs. They, and I, simply had different ideologies and some of them, like the prisoner in the first chapter, certainly had reasons to think differently than me.

As for the average South Vietnamese peasant, he did not love the Americans, nor did he love the Communists, and/or the North Vietnamese. He loved his family, his way of life, and wanted to be left alone so that he might plow his fields and do as he pleased. Unfortunately, for thousands of years, other nations have never been able to leave him alone to do so.

I have tried to be as open and honest as possible in this book in the hope that through it one might achieve a better understanding of one aspect of the Viet Nam War, the country of Viet Nam, some of the people of that country, and one United States soldier's role in that war.

The thing to keep in mind as you read this is that I am telling you what I saw, felt, smelled, and heard. You are getting one side only. I am not a military strategist, I am not a politician, I have no "axe to grind", and I am not even trying to make money. I am certainly not trying to make myself out to be a hero or an exceptionally brave or smart soldier. I was certainly none of those.

I have had military "experts" read this and tell me that such and such could/would not have happened in Viet Nam. In one instance one such expert wrote me that the US Medevac helicopters never picked up Vietnamese civilians for treatment. He said, "That was totally against U.S. policy, and it did not happen."

I did not argue. I simply know that it did happen in my District. Maybe it did not happen elsewhere. I am not disputing military roles, rules, or procedures. I am simply telling what happened with me during my year in Viet Nam. I am sure that many of the veterans who read this can relate to many things they were told, "did not happen" in their areas of operation.

In my opinion, the U.S. did not do everything right in the Viet Nam war. We probably did not do everything right in any war in which we have fought. But, the soldiers who served their country in those wars have every right to proud of that service.

Chapter 3
THE PHOENIX PROGRAM

Contrary to what you might imagine, my first flight to South Viet Nam was actually very pleasant. The large Braniff was comfortable, the food was good, and the stewardesses were considerate, sympathetic, and very attractive in their brightly colored uniforms that matched the décor of the plane.

However, I did feel a little cheated. According to every movie I had ever seen about men going to war, the hero was supposed to maintain a dramatic Napoleonic posture and wear a scowl. I tried to assume the correct, professional, James Bond pose, but my mind kept flashing movies of my last few days with my wife, and I caught myself smiling rather than maintaining the required scowl. Finally, I gave up and went to the back of the plane where a number of the guys were playing poker. I ended up having a good time and even the loss of a few dollars failed to ruin a very enjoyable flight.

Our landing and debarkation in Cam Rahn Bay was not pleasant, or exciting, or dramatic. It was dull, boring, and again completely unlike what I'm sure we all had imagined.

I had pictured that I would be landing in a wild melee of mortar rounds, explosions, machine gun fire, grenades being thrown, and people screaming. In fact, I had imagined a wild cacophony of sound, light, and terror.

What I got was long lines that endlessly weaved around and around the wooden benches in a make shift waiting room, while a lone Corporal tried to straighten out the paperwork of 200 Second Lieutenants.

Had I been more alert to the paper shuffling being done behind the desk, I would have picked up my first clue as to the fact that some of us were being reassigned. As it turned out, I didn't wise up to the Army's stalling tactics for three days and by then everyone knew that something was going on.

We were being kept in Cam Rahn and were not sent immediately to our units. *Why?* Was the question we all began asking, but no one could, or would, give us an answer. Everyone we asked confirmed the fact that new Lieutenants were usually sent straight to their assigned units; but, for some reason, some of us had been singled out and required to stay put for a few days.

Lt. Jones was a guy I had met while I was in Jungle School in Panama and he was, like me, a basketball junkie. So, he and I spent most of our time playing basketball on an outdoor court and lying in our bunks talking about our homes, while some of the guys took out motor boats for water skiing in the Bay. That's right, water skiing in Cam Rahn Bay. It was certainly not the dramatic entrance into a war zone that we had expected.

Lt. Green, a real nut whom I will talk about later, was the first to bring news of our transfers, but he was always "blowing smoke", and no one ever listened to him. However, when he showed us the orders tacked to the bulletin board, we were convinced.

One hundred and seventy of our flight were to leave the next day for their original assignments, while about twenty of us – the only college graduates of the group – were not told when we would be leaving or where we would be going. Under the word assignment, the 4th. Infantry Division has been crossed out and the word "Confidential" had been written.

Here we were, in Viet Nam, apprehensive, scared, obviously a little confused, and then the Army places the word Confidential next to our names in the column marked assignment. You think that did not raise our eyebrows even further? No one would tell us anything for two days, and then we were just told to board a plane.

On the plane, instead of the word Confidential, we started hearing the word PHOENIX. We were told that, no, we were not going to

Phoenix, Arizona. PHOENIX was the name of the program to which we had been assigned, but none of us had ever heard of it.

Personally I did not care where we went or what we did as long as we did something. I was bored. The waiting had taken its toll on my nerves and I needed something to take my mind off of my wife, home, and the empty feeling I had inside. There seems to be an odd, thin line between bravery, cowardice, and the simple relief of boredom.

After we had been in the air for an hour we were told we were being flown to Saigon. We didn't know what we were going to do, but Saigon sounded like the place to be doing something. Oh, the stories we had heard about that city! After we had been in the jungle for a few months its very name would conjure up dreams of indescribably delicious steaks, ice cream, flushing toilets, cool drinks, and for the single guys (and many of the married ones), beautiful women. But, to us then, it simply meant the excitement of the unknown and the escape from the jungles of Pleiku where the 4th Infantry was deployed.

Again, however, our dreams did not fit the reality. We were not allowed the freedoms of the city. We were literally locked inside a compound in Saigon and our days were filled with lectures on counterinsurgency, guerilla warfare, and a surprising amount of what can only be described as political brainwashing.

The term PHOENIX was used repeatedly and after a week of concentrated study we learned the full implications of the word, as it would apply to us. We also learned why this particular "pacification program" was labeled Confidential. At the time, had the American public learned the sorted details of its operation, the anti-war rallyists would really have had something to rally round.

The CIA it seems, had decided that the communist elements in South Vietnam were becoming too strong. These elements, "Vietnamese Cadre Infrastructure or VCI", as Saigon called them, were setting up shadow governments in most of the hamlets, villages, and provinces in the country. These shadow governments collected taxes, recruited soldiers for the Viet Cong, spent time military proselytizing, and doing all the political maneuvering that a real government would do. The US political powers were evidently afraid that should a coalition government be established, as was the theory during the time of PHOENIX, the National Liberation Front would have their shadow governments step into the light and claim governmental control over their respective areas. If the country was to be divided according to the areas controlled, these maneuverings would definitely strengthen the communist claims of authority and power.

The CIA was assigned, or possibly thought up themselves, the task of eliminating or "neutralizing" these communist elements. In other words, these civilians needed to be assassinated or captured, thus the PHOENIX program was born.

We learned that our jobs as PHOENIX coordinators would be to go into a district, set up a district intelligence base to collect information on these individuals, then send out special patrols to capture or eliminate them. We were to be given great sums of money to pay informants throughout the district and given the authority to set up an assembly center for all intelligence elements in the district: Korean, American, and Vietnamese. The center was called a DIOCC - District Intelligence Operation and Coordinating Center.

Finally, as a "coup de grace" we were to be supplied with the proper group of soldiers to carry out such an unconventional program. These soldiers had no political preference and no loyalties. They were cruel, merciless, and faithful to whoever paid them the most. They were in fact mercenaries. Later in 1968 an American magazine contained an article which unearthed the PHOENIX program and in it these soldiers were called, "the butchers of Viet Nam." But, to us then, they were an unknown, but obviously deadly commodity.

Saigon told us they were called, PRU - Provincial Reconnaissance Units - but the Vietnamese called the "Biet Kick". I never did learn what Biet Kick meant in Vietnamese, but an American Colonel later told me that it must mean something like the American expression, "Kicking Butt", because that is what they did to every unit that was unfortunate enough to tangle with them. Regardless of their name, they were one of the most effective, most efficient, and most feared forces to ever fight in Viet Nam, or anywhere else for that matter.

Unlike some other special US units, who were famous for insane charges up insignificant hills, or for establishing outposts in areas that no one wanted anyway, the PRU were supposed to strike at the enemy's head. They bypassed the foot soldier. They made no crazy charges, and spent no time on senseless fortifications. The 14 year old kid with a rifle was often left alone. The PRU searched out and neutralized his master, the man who gave him and fifty of his friends their orders. While other forces were concentrating on killing the kids in Viet Nam, the kids who were deadly and did indeed kill a lot of our soldiers, but who would not be instrumental in the outcome of the war, the PRU were tracking down and eliminating the power elements in the country: The communist civilians who were trying to take over South Viet Nam.

The PRU's tactics were far from conventional, their behavior often barbaric and inhumane, their patriotism questionable, but they efficiently and effectively carried out the missions assigned to them by the DIOCC coordinators. One of whom I had been assigned to be.

These were the troops that the other new lieutenants and I were assigned to equip, pay, and "control". We were to use them to eliminate or neutralize the VCI in our respective Districts.

In Saigon jargon, neutralize meant to capture. The idea being that once captured, one VCI could be convinced to divulge pertinent information concerning the names, locations, and movements of other VCI. This sounded great while we were sitting in the comparative safety of meetings in a compound in Saigon, and before I got out into the jungles, entirely possible. However, once I got into the jungles, reality set in. Just because something sounds good, and looks good on paper, doesn't mean that it will work the same way in the real world. It was like a lot of the ideas and principles I heard during the education classes in college. They sounded good, but in the real world of the classroom, many of them simply did not work.

Again, all of this was relayed to us during days of speeches in a locked compound in Saigon. Then, finally, we were taken to a DIOCC that had already been set up in one of the districts just outside of Saigon. It was all very confusing and I really had no specific ideas as to what was going on or what I was supposed to exactly do if they dropped me off in a district of my own.

Unfortunately, the Army had no time for my doubts and the very next day my worst fears were realized. Some of us were loaded aboard a plane and flown to Pleiku. Pleiku is where the 4th Infantry was stationed and where I was supposed to be a front line platoon leader. It is in the mountains, set amid miles and miles of thick triple canopy jungle. For an outdoorsman, it would be a wonderful place to hike, be a birdwatcher, and live a mountain man's life. During war, it had to be a nightmare for both sides.

We got off the plane and were taken to a DIOCC that had been established there. One of members of our group was to take over control of this area, so this was to be his home for the next year. We were shown around his new facilities, explanations of what was going on were given to us, and then we were taken back to the plane - more confused than when we had gotten off.

We were flown to five other locations around the country until there were only five of us left on the plane. At the Tuy Hoa Air Force Base we were told to disembark and immediately load our things onto a waiting helicopter. This copter took us to the Army post in Tuy Hoa. There we were picked up by an American civilian named Clarkson, who was the head of the PHOENIX program in II Corps, and taken in an old Ford station wagon to a large, stucco house which was surrounded by concertina wire and guard posts.

The other four guys were taken to their respective districts, which were close to the city. However, Clarkson explained that since I was a little older (I was 25 at the time) than some of the guys, I had been given a special posting in Tuy An. He said that the District Chief there was the most powerful, opinionated, ruthless, and yet probably most successful one in all of Viet Nam. He said that I had my job cut out for me and he wished me luck. He muttered something to the effect that I would need it. He then said that the road leading to my district had been heavily mined so I would have to go by helicopter and that one was not readily available.

24

I was happy for the delay because of my confusion as to what I was actually supposed to do when I got there, and I let Clarkson know what I was worrying about. He laughed and said he totally understood. Then he tried to allay my worries by explaining the basic principles of my job.

He said that my troops were already in Tuy An, and that they had an experienced leader in a guy named Hung. An American Lieutenant had preceded me to the district and the DIOCC had already been set up. My responsibilities were to see to it that informants were paid, to receive their information, to collate all this information, and then to use this information to direct my troops to neutralize the opposition. He said that the PHOENIX program was made up of guidelines and I was simply supposed to use the guidelines, my own common sense, and to do the best I could at carrying out the general idea of the program. He made it sound very simple.

Clarkson was a civilian and I realized as I talked to him that he was in a very ticklish situation. Here he was, giving orders and instructions to a military officer and basically telling me that my job was to target and eliminate other civilians. This was definitely not covered in the Uniform Code of Military Justice. If this program blew up, or if I caused some problems in the district, it would all fall back on him - and on me of course. The CIA was certainly not going to even acknowledge my existence, and certainly not their connection to such a program. Nice to know that your backside is covered - right?

Clarkson assured me that I would have a tremendous amount of freedom in how I ran my operation in the district, but he was adamant about my following his orders specifically on two points: I was never to go against the District Chief's orders, and I was to protect my files at all costs. He assured me that these two areas would cause me more soul searching agony than I could imagine. I, of course, had no idea what he was talking about, but told him I would protect the files and that if my orders were that I was to obey the District Chief, then of course I would. He just smiled at my ignorance, and to what I was so freely agreeing to do.

The next day I met Hung, my Vietnamese mercenary leader. He was about 5'5", his skin was a dark muddy color, and his hair was coal black.

It is really hard for me to explain, over 44 years after having met him, but there was something terribly frightening about him. Something ugly and evil seemed to lurk behind his eyes, even when he was smiling at you. I explained earlier that Be's eyes seemed normal enough until he got very angry and turned into a madman. Then his eyes enlarged and glowed. Hung was entirely different in that he never looked normal.

Recently Joeline and I were at an animal park in Guatemala. A jaguar was in a cage not a foot from me. He stood at the wire and stared at me. I could have been staring into Hung's eyes. They were the eyes of a predator. Hung's eyes were not black like most of the Vietnamese, his were a jungle green. They were large, he hardly ever blinked, and he could see in the dark like no one I have ever met.

Most people explained that they were always afraid when they were around him; that fear superimposed itself over whatever they were trying to do when he was near. Luckily, the reverse was true for me. I always felt totally safe when he was near, although I had to constantly watch out for the safety of others when he was with me. It was like having a loyal pet Bengal Tiger beside me. I felt secure, but had to constantly be on the watch to see that he did not take the arm off of someone who was simply trying to hand me a glass of water.

He was the perfect mercenary soldier in all respects but one. He was ruthless, had no conscience whatsoever, was extremely protective of his men's welfare, was both loved and feared by them, and had an almost uncanny knowledge and feel for the jungle. However, he hated the Viet Cong with such an unreasoning passion that there was never any danger of his turning against us and working for them - this, of course, was great for me, but it was not the mark of a true mercenary.

When I met him he was in Tuy Hoa to try and get new uniforms for his men and himself. It all worked out very well for me because I had been issued twenty five sets of jungle fatigues to give to my new unit. Hung was impressed that I had gone to the trouble of getting them, and I didn't bother telling him that they weren't my idea.

I wanted to hitch a ride with him to Tuy An, but he politely told the interpreter that it was not possible. I assumed that he wanted to be the

26

hero with the rest of the PRU by bringing back the new uniforms, and if I were along he probably felt that I would hog the glory for myself. Later I found out that that was not the case. Hung could have cared less about who got credit for anything. He was simply looking out for my welfare. He had been told, by an informant, that he was the target of an assassination attempt and he did not want to endanger my life by having me ride with him. Plus, he knew that I was new, extremely green, and he might have been afraid as to how I would react in a pressure situation if he was attacked. He also knew that if I was killed while with him, he would be in a lot of trouble with Saigon.

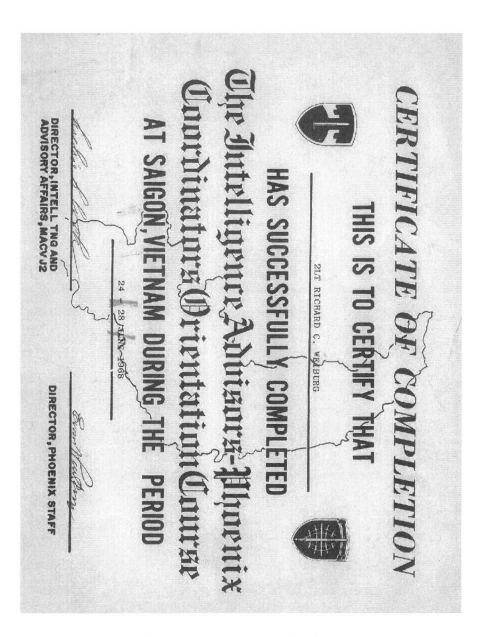

Phoenix Course Completion Certificate

Chapter 4
FIRST PRISONERS

As it turned out, I finally had to take a jeep to Tuy An. No chopper was available and Clarkson said I needed to get out there. He felt that Highway One was not as bad as the reports had evidently made it out to be, so he put me in a jeep with his driver and a bodyguard and sent me on my way.

I can't remember too much about my first ride to my new home, except that it seemed a long way. I do recall rounding a curve on a small hill and the driver pointing out the compound a few miles away. The compound was small, with only four buildings. It was totally surrounded by four different rows of concertina wire and two sets of trenches. There seemed to be only one way in or out and that was through the front gate. (A couple of months later the District Chief and I were to get in a big argument about that before I finally managed to get him to engineer an escape route out the back of the compound through the mine field.)

The driver dropped me off just inside the compound and headed back to Tuy Hoa. Now, I was on my own in Viet Nam. I was not a member of a large American unit. I did not have a Colonel, Major, or even a Captain to look out for me or tell me what I should or should not do. I didn't speak Vietnamese, I didn't know anyone, and I had no idea what I should do first. I was in charge of a mercenary squad. I was in charge of 20 men who had been trained to, and whose job it was to do one thing, kill people. A few days before that, I had been with my wife in Fresno, California. What a difference a few days make.

I walked into the building that had a large MACV emblem painted on the side. Introductions were short and I didn't remember any of the six or seven names I was given. There was a Colonel there, who was in charge of the MACV team, a Captain under his control, along with a sergeant, and several corporals.

MACV, stood for Military Assistance Command, Vietnam. These people were in the District to aid/assist/advise the Vietnamese forces in their fight against the Viet Cong. They were there to help the Vietnamese, not to do the fighting for them. I was not assigned to any of the officers. I was not a part of MACV. I was basically my own boss.

The building had a small room at the front which served as a lounge and radio room. A hall led directly down the middle to the kitchen at the rear. On each side of the hall were five small cubicles with a curtain serving as a door on each. I was given the first one on the left. It was the least desirable as it was closest to the lounge and there was the constant noise of the radio going all night. I was the new guy, so I got the worst cubicle, just the way it should be.

By the time I was finished unpacking, dinner was being served. The cooking was shared by each of the seven Americans in the compound. The food was edible, though certainly not good. There was no fresh meat or vegetables. Most items were either dried or powdered - such as eggs, potatoes, and milk - or canned, like spam.

After eating I went outside the building and watched the preparations of a compound at war getting ready for the night. I can sleep anywhere and anytime and after turning in, had no trouble falling asleep that first night. However, I was awakened by a tremendous explosion that nearly knocked me out of my cot. I grabbed my carbine and ran out into the lounge area in my shorts. The man on duty just grinned and asked what had taken me so long.

The noise was simply the 155mm Howitzers, which were positioned on each side of the building, firing at the hills to the west of us. It seems that the South Vietnamese Artillery Unit in the compound fired on the same hills every night to keep the VC from setting mortars up there and firing at us. I told the Corporal who was on radio duty that he might have let me know. He said, "What fun would that have been?" It was evidently traditional not to mention it to any new men. The next morning at breakfast I was obviously going to be the brunt of the jokes.

These nightly firings shook the building unmercifully, but after a few nights I got used to them and they never woke me again.

I walked out of the building the next morning, walked across the compound to a separate building that had DIOCC painted on the side, and entered my office. The building actually had two offices. One was mine and the other was for the Vietnamese soldiers who were actually given the informant reports. They took them, read them, placed an English translation at the bottom, and then put them on my desk. (A copy also went to the District Chief.)

I asked one of the soldiers in the other office to find my interpreter, whom I had been told was a Vietnamese boy named Gem. When Gem showed up, I asked him to find Hung. When they both came in I told Hung, through Gem, to do what he thought was necessary with the PRU for the next few days while I got my feet on the ground and found out what we should be doing. I suggested he check with Dai Uy Be before doing too much.

They both laughed as my interpreter repeated this, and I was told that no one did anything in the district without checking with the District Chief first. This was my first lesson in regard to Dai Uy Be.

A few days later Hung and a couple of the PRU captured two men who were reportedly VCI during an operation Be had set up for them. The captures were not particularly important or memorable, and the captured men eventually turned out not to be VCI, they were just ordinary VC foot soldiers. I would not even recall the incident except for the fact that it brought down on me the wrath of Be, the guy of whom I had heard so much, and probably the most feared District Chief in all of Viet Nam.

Be ruled a territory that would be the equivalent of one of our Counties. And, when I say ruled it, I mean just that. He could do as he pleased in Tuy An District and no one in that district would ever question his actions.

31

He always walked around with a pair of pearl handled 45's on his hips, like he was a sheriff from some old western movie - although the guns in the westerns would have been Colt revolvers. Anyway, on more than one occasion during my year there, I watched him pull one of those pistols out and blow a prisoner's head off. He was to be feared because he was half crazy and yet, he was very intelligent. This is a very dangerous combination, and an extremely volatile one.

Part of my job was to keep the Province Headquarters in Tuy Hoa informed of any "eliminations" (kills), or "neutralizations"(captures) that occurred in the district: if they were VCI. If they were not VCI then the responsibility of reporting rested with the ranking Army officer in the compound - there was usually a Colonel in that position. So, when I heard that the PRU had the two men, who were suspected of being VCI, I immediately notified my superiors in Tuy Hoa. I couldn't give them much information, but assured them that I would get back to them with the prisoners' names and job titles as soon as possible.

I then tried to get to the prisoners to interrogate them, but found that Be had taken them to his underground bunker, along with Hung, whom he used as his interrogator. The commanding Army officer in the compound at that time was Colonel Kolb and he informed me that the interrogation bunker was off limits to all U.S. personnel, unless expressly invited by Be.

It may seem strange that the PRU, who were technically under my command, had taken the prisoners to Be, but remember we were in Viet Nam and Be was the Vietnamese District Chief. It was his district and whatever happened in it was his responsibility. If I had been in an American compound, with an American unit, things would have been totally different. But, as it was, I was only an advisor to the Vietnamese. I still did not like the situation, and I wasted no time in telling Be so when we finally did talk.

A few days later Dai Uy Be called me into his office, offered me tea, and then apologized for not conferring with me before interrogating the prisoners that my PRU had captured. He said that since originally they were thought to be VCI, I should have been involved. I sat back, relaxed, and wondered why people feared this very reasonable sounding man. Then his expression changed. Although he spoke very broken English, he made it very clear to me that if I ever again sent a report anywhere concerning anything that took place in his district without first clearing it with him, I would immediately be forced to leave his district. And, he made it very clear that I would probably not be standing when I left.

We stared at each other for a few seconds. Then I told him that I accepted his apology and that I agreed with him that I should have contacted him before sending in my report. I made it very clear that my superiors had told me that I was to do whatever the district chief said and I planned to obey my orders.

He smiled and figured he had won a total victory and that I was just going to be an American lackey whom he could easily push around and "manage" as he saw fit.

However, I then proceeded to explain that although I would tell him before I sent any radio or written communications through normal Army channels, and although I would let him dictate to some extent what was in those reports, as long as there were no lies, that I also would, with or without his permission, send a factual report to my superior in the PHOENIX program concerning everything that went on in the district. I said that I would send that report through confidential channels so that only Clarkson saw it. What Clarkson would do with the reports I did not know and had no control over, but I had to, and would send him the reports. I told Be that if that was not good enough, then I would appreciate it if he would get me transferred out of the District as soon as possible.

I smiled, and said, "While I'm still standing." I laughed and told him I did not want to go the other way, and so I was being entirely up front and honest with him.

He stared at me for a moment and then broke into a huge smile. He said, "We get along fine. You send only truth to Army, only maybe leave out some things that I tell you, but you send whole truth to Mr. Clarkson. He good man. He know Dai Uy Be. You and I be real friends, not just GI and Vietnamese. You have more tea?"

33

As far as these particular prisoners went, I found out the problem. Only one of them made it through the interrogation alive, and even he would not be sent on to Tuy Hoa or Saigon. So, when Be's superiors in Saigon asked where the two prisoners were, Be would have to make up some story about how they were killed while trying to escape. It was an embarrassing situation for Be and he did not like to be embarrassed.

I got the message. Not every prisoner we captured would be sent on through military channels. In fact, as far as I, or any of my reports to the Army were concerned, no one was actually captured until Be said so. However, I reported absolutely everything of importance that happened to Clarkson. I have no idea how much of this he forwarded through Army channels.

As it turned out, we hardly ever had a problem in this regard. Although my DIOCC led all of Viet Nam in the number of VCI killed each month, we seldom had any prisoners, much to the dismay and frustration of my superiors. They loved my kill count, but they wanted prisoners.

Captures were minimal for two reasons:

First, most of the VCI we were after moved around only at night. They stayed in their own secured areas during the day to avoid detection. They went out at night to do their governmental work under the cover of darkness. Thus, the PRU could usually only set up their ambushes to try to "capture" these people at night, and capturing someone at night in a jungle is a very difficult and dangerous business.

Let me give you an example of a typical PRU ambush. Let's say that I would get information that Tru Tuan was the Communist finance chief of Phu Duct Hamlet and that he visited the members of that hamlet every Tuesday night to collect taxes. After getting enough informant reports to confirm this information, I would send the PRU out on a Tuesday night to set up ambushes along as many of the trails leading into that particular hamlet as possible.

Anyone who has been in a jungle knows that this is a ticklish business. There are many trails leading into a hamlet, so I had to divide the PRU into 3 to 5 man cells to try to cover as many trails as possible.

Important VCI traveled well protected with up to 30 bodyguards, and when this contingent of enemy forces walked into an ambush it would have been suicidal for the PRU to stand up and yell: "Hands up, we've got you covered!" in Vietnamese of course. The outcome of that folly would be that the whole body of men would melt into the jungle and escape or they would attack the ambush and probably kill all of my men.

Everyone in Vietnam, including women and children, knew that walking around a jungle at night was suicidal. Jungles were considered free-fire zones at night. Anything that moved in the jungle at night could be shot with no questions asked and no warning given.

When anything walked into a PRU ambush, the men in the cell would open up with everything they had: M-1's, (later they had M-16's), hand grenades, AK 47's, and the claymore mines that were hopefully available. Then the members of the cell would withdraw to prearranged spots and wait for dawn. If they were in a relatively secure area, they would check the ambush site at first light to see what they had got. If they were not certain of the safety of going back to the site, they would withdraw and wait for the jungle grapevine to bring them news of any "kills", or, we would take a heavy patrol to the site the next day.

Usually the ambushers sat out all night and got nothing. Occasionally, unfortunately, they killed "innocents" who were where they should not have been, and sometimes they got who I had actually targeted. Sometimes the noise that triggered the ambush turned out to be a stray water buffalo. One time I was with an ambush team and we mistakenly attacked the leading elements of an entire North Vietnamese Regiment, but that is another story.

The second reason the PRU took few prisoners was because early in the program, before I arrived, they had been betrayed by their own country's system of justice. In 1968, when the program began, they captured a few very important VCI. These men were sent to Saigon for interrogation and trial. Unfortunately, these men were very wealthy and influential and they simply bought their way out of trouble and were soon back in the district doing business as usual and laughing at the effort of the PRU and Dai Uy Be.

The PRU and Be learned to interrogate their own prisoners. The populace learned that if a prisoner was lucky enough to make it to Saigon and then lucky enough to get back to Tuy An, that man was an endangered species if he ever so much as thought of stepping out of line again.

Chapter 5
THE CRIPPLE

The finger of fate was forever randomly selecting victims in Viet Nam. The good and the bad were equally susceptible to its deadly touch. I found one such victim of circumstance while acting as an advisor to a combined task force of Korean and South Vietnamese soldiers.

My PRU's were taking a few days off, so I got the brilliant idea of putting together a combined Korean/South Vietnamese operation. I thought I knew where a small group of VC were hiding, and I mistakenly, as it turned out, felt we could surround and capture them.

Although there was a ROK (Republic of Korea) compound in the district, they hardly ever did anything. I wanted to get them involved in at least trying to eliminate VC in the district, so I had one of my mercenaries who spoke Korean, go to their compound and talk to their commander. The Korean commander, Kim, actually owed me a favor because a couple of weeks before, I had kept a couple of his soldiers from getting killed by Be and touching off an international incident:

> Two Koreans had come into our compound on some mission from their post, but stayed and got drunk with a couple of Be's men. Be's men were smart enough to stay out of sight, and keep quiet, but the Koreans started running around the compound shouting and firing their rifles up in the air. Of course all the Americans grabbed their weapons and ran out ready for combat. Then we saw what was going on and just enjoyed the

spectacle. We had no idea what the Koreans were yelling, but it sounded funny. One of my guys later told me that they were shouting Korean profanities, but he wouldn't get more specific. He said they were really bad words. Anyway, they were dancing around in the middle of the compound and I was reminded of a bunch of Apaches doing some sort of war dance. As long as their rifles stayed pointed in the air we were all getting an afternoon's entertainment. We welcomed anything to relieve the monotony of long hours in the compound. Then Dai Uy Be walked out of his hut and it was obvious he was just going to shoot the idiots. I intervened, convinced Be that they were harmless and even got him to smile a little. Then I got the two guys, who were by now staggering and about to fall down, into my jeep and drove them to the Korean compound. Kim knew he owed me for their lives. But more importantly, I saved both compounds a lot of trouble and loss of face.

The problems with the ROK forces in our District really bothered and surprised me. They certainly were not acting, behaving, or performing like the Koreans with whom I had dealt in the past. I went to high school in the San Joaquin Valley in California. (This was after attending 36 different schools all over the United States from grade one through eight because of my family's moving with the race horses.) Anyway, in my high school there were many Koreans and their work ethics were far superior to mine. They worked harder in school, after school, and in sports. They were extremely courteous, honorable, and intelligent. Most of the Koreans I had known were truly over achievers.

In some of the other Districts in Viet Nam, my counterparts told me that the ROK's were the best soldiers in their areas. I have no idea why the unit in our District was so bad, but it was, and it was a discredit to the Korean soldiers as a whole.

So, while my man was talking to the Korean commander I went to Be to try to sell him on the idea of actually working with the Koreans.

He was very hesitant at first, but finally agreed to set up a patrol. I really felt he agreed too easily and later found out why he had done so.

I put a plan together and since neither Be nor Kim would turn control of their troops over to anyone else, I had to treat the two units separately, each with their own commander and their own sets of orders. I quickly found that neither group would move ahead of the other for fear of being shot, so I had to divide them and send the Koreans in a circling operation one way and the Vietnamese the other. We were to encircle this small area where I believed some VC to be, and then try to take everyone inside the circle, as prisoners. I was simply going along as an observer and since I felt I could communicate enough with both troops to get along on this short patrol, I did not even bother to take an interpreter along.

The operation got underway much later than I had hoped, but since these two groups had never worked together, I suppose that was to be expected. It only took me a short time, and a couple of kilometers, to realize that the entire operation was going to be a total bust.

Shortly after we started, I heard gunfire from the general area where the Koreans were traveling and immediately had to send a runner to the area to find out what was going on.

Clack had our radio tuned to a frequency the Colonel was monitoring, the Koreans had their own radios tuned to their frequency, and the Vietnamese had a radio tuned to a channel that Di Uy Be was monitoring. To call the Koreans by radio, I would have to call the Colonel, have him call them by way of a land line, find out what was going on, and then radio me back. So, it was much easier for me to simply send a runner.

I found that the Koreans were not under any kind of attack and had not encountered VC, they were simply shooting birds to eat with the balls of rice that they were going to have for lunch. They were obviously not interested in encountering any Viet Cong.

The Vietnamese troops I was with were making so much noise that it was also evident that they were just out for a walk and did not plan to get involved in any firefight with the Viet Cong. Any VC within miles would have left the area.

I understood the situation. The Korean commander and Be had both given me what I asked for, but neither of them liked me getting involved in their "war". Maybe they thought I was trying to usurp their power. Anyway, it was plain that they thought I should stick to my own guerrilla war and leave them to the large unit tactics. They had obviously told their troop leaders to go, but to stay out of any trouble.

So, for half a day we walked through a secure section of the District while the troops talked, joked, shot birds, and in every way they could, had an enjoyable time. Of course I was furious at Be and Kim, but quickly resolved myself to the fact that it was their war and if that was the way they wanted to fight it, then I might as well relax and enjoy the walk. The Vietnamese commander was smart enough to keep us in an area secure from any large ambush, so I made myself as safe as possible and began to enjoy the countryside and the chance to be out in it during the daylight hours. Up to this point, most of my time had been spent on ambushes in the middle of the night.

Possibly I had better explain my statement, "as safe as possible". First, I did not walk next to Clack, the American radio operator. VC snipers learned early in the war that American officers walked next to their radio man. So, Clack walked with two Vietnamese soldiers and I kept a few others between us. Second, I walked far enough into the column to avoid any mines we might encounter. I did not wear any rank insignia on my jungle fatigues and made myself as unobtrusive as I could, considering the fact that I had blond hair, blue eyes and was much taller than all the Vietnamese.

This may sound cowardly, but I did not look at it that way. The life expectancy of a Lieutenant, as I have said was very short, and when you consider the nightly ambushes I was going out on almost constantly, mine was even less than most. By being extremely careful on operations like this, I was simply trying to lengthen the odds against me. I was no coward, nor was I a hero. My aim in Viet Nam was to keep my men and myself alive, and to do my job. Everything else, including heroics, I could do without. The odds were against us all and I tried to pad mine as much as possible.

40

I knew Be would not have sent the men out at all unless he had something to gain from it. I assumed he knew we would see no VC but needed to give these troops some exercise and the commander a chance to lead the men. The old "itching palm" that Cassius was accused of in Julius Caesar was very prevalent in Viet Nam. In many districts it was common practice to buy one's way into a prominent military position. However, to be perfectly fair, I do not believe Be would put an unproven commander in charge of a "hot" operation, regardless of the money involved. This was simply meant to be a learning experience for the commander.

We were walking through a small hamlet when a commotion arose in one of the huts. A woman screamed and began shouting. Two of our soldiers appeared in the doorway of the hut and threw a small boy, approximately 11 years old, into the dirt. Then they began to savagely kick him while he tried unsuccessfully to protect his head, stomach, and groin.

I assumed that we had run across a bunch of VC and began to look around for the rest. But soon it was obvious that this one small boy was the extent of the "enemy" in the hamlet.

Two more soldiers were coming out of the hut when the woman who had been screaming rushed up behind them. She tried to get past them to aid the boy, probably her son, but one of the soldiers responded by swinging a rifle butt into her face. She was knocked back into the hut with blood streaming down from her nose and mouth.

The boy was yanked to his feet, or rather I should say, yanked to his one foot. He had only one leg. He was pushed into our line of march and was forced to hop enough to keep up as the unit started off. It was immediately evident that he was not going to be able to keep up and I started toward the company commander. Before I reached him, a young girl ran out of the back of a hut carrying a crutch. She risked the wrath of the soldiers by running up and handing the crutch to the boy. With it, he was able to stay ahead of the soldier behind him, and thus avoid a poke in the back with a bayonet.

41

We walked aimlessly for the next few hours and accomplished nothing. The boy fell a few times and was rewarded with swift kicks and a lot of swearing.

I went up to the boy several times and tried to get him to let me help him. Clack and I were even going to try to carry him, but he wanted nothing to do with us. He spat and swore and tried to hit us with his crutch every time we went near him. He seemed to hate us far worse than he did the Vietnamese who were basically "torturing" him.

The soldiers thought it was really funny when he tried to hit me with the crutch and suggested that I shoot him. They would point to him and say, "VC, VC, you kill. OK, no problem".

By two in the afternoon we were back in the compound. I was hot, dirty, and tired. The six hour walk had ceased to be a pleasant experience for me once we had picked up the boy, and the two hours he had been with us must have been pure hell for him. I immediately sent for Gem and told him I wanted a full explanation as to what the boy had done, or was being accused of having done. Gem had not seen us come in and thus had no idea who I was talking about. He left to find out.

He came back a few seconds later. He knew the boy by sight and knew his story. It seems that the boy's father had been an active Viet Cong and had even had some training in Hanoi. The boy, at the age of eight, had begun to help his father. One day he received a bit of news that would forever change his life. He learned that there was an ambush being set up near the area where he knew his father would be traveling.

The boy left his village as soon as he could and raced to warn the man he loved and admired. It was just dark when he caught up with his father. Unfortunately, he caught his dad at precisely the wrong time and place. The ambush was sprung. The father and several other men were killed and the boy was seriously wounded. He was eventually taken to Tuy Hoa as a prisoner of war and his leg was amputated due to the wounds he had received during the ambush.

A few months later he was released. But released to do what? His father was dead, his own leg was gone, and he was branded by his countrymen as a VC. He returned to Tuy An a bitter young boy who hated the government forces and their American allies. It was a totally understandable attitude.

Where the South Vietnamese government saw in him a militarily useless child, the Viet Cong saw a valuable commodity and lost no time in again enlisting his aid. If anyone hated the government and the Americans as much as the boy did, then the VC would find a use for him.

Was he physically dangerous? Absolutely, he was certainly capable of setting off mines and pulling the trigger on a rifle. Just because he was handicapped did not mean that he could not kill. But, the VC knew he could be put to much better use.

They used him as a propaganda device to help them collect taxes and to help gain sympathy for their cause. He was taken to a different hamlet each night with a group of VC and he would tell the villagers how he and his father had been attacked, without cause, by the bloodthirsty government and the American butchers.

Be evidently knew of the boys activities, but he had given orders, for some reason, that the boy not be killed. I suppose Be felt that his murder would only help the cause of the VC. But, then again, Be rarely cared what anyone thought.

So, the boy was periodically taken from his home, beaten, warned to stop working for the VC, and then released.

I saw the boy leave the compound the next morning. He was small and dirty. His clothes were torn, and obviously his gait was irregular. However, he held himself with a bearing and dignity that he did not physically seem to deserve. I realized why many of the South Vietnamese soldiers hated him. He managed to maintain his honor, character, and self-respect, and they could not stand that, much less understand it.

I often wonder what eventually happened to the boy. The North Vietnamese took control of the country and he had done so much for their cause. I hope he lived through the war and was then given the respect he seemed to deserve.

This was taken not long after the capture of the "Great Enemy"!
He is the kid with only one leg on the far right in the picture.

Chapter 6

HUNG'S CAVE

The United States government spent thousands of dollars on a "Chu Hoa" program. This program was designed to tempt Viet Cong guerillas into giving up and coming over to the side of the South Vietnamese government. Those who did "come over" were given money, their crimes were forgiven, and they were offered a job, usually as a South Vietnamese soldier. These Chu Hoas were expected to give the authorities the names, locations, and hiding places of other Viet Cong in the area.

I did not expect this program to be any more successful than my wanted posters. (I will talk about them in a later chapter.) But, as I was not associated with the Chu Hoa program I cannot provide any positive facts regarding its success or failure. However, one Viet Cong did "defect" in our area and gave us some very useful information.

We knew that there was a supply line which originated in Hanoi, passed through the deep jungle in our district, and ended up somewhere near Saigon. We also felt that it passed through an area which we called VC Valley. This section of Tuy An District was not safe. It was a free fire area, meaning anything that moved there was considered the enemy.

It was an area of deep, triple canopy jungle. An area where an entire North Vietnamese Regiment could easily move, sleep, or camp, and never be afraid of being spotted by American aircraft; and according to all the information I could gather, often did. To initiate an operation into this area with the small number of forces available to me was unhealthy, unwise, and in fact suicidal.

We had called air strikes into the area on several occasions when I received enough evidence to warrant doing so, but sending jets to drop bombs into a huge jungle like that was like throwing rocks in an ocean hoping to hit and kill a whale.

The Chu Hoa who came in, insisted that he had been brought down from North Viet Nam as a member of a resupply party. He had been left near a cave with a few other guys and told to guard it. After being left out in the jungle for months he was tired of the entire ordeal. He had been a teacher in North Vietnam before he was "recruited", and he felt the South Vietnamese would place him in a more civilized environment.

According to him, the cave contained food supplies, blankets, and ammo. Basically, anything a North Vietnamese soldier might need on his long trip from Hanoi to Saigon. At one time there had been over 5,000 soldiers billeted in the jungle around the cave, but he indicated that the cave had not been resupplied for some time and that they were starting to run short of some items.

After much debate, he consented to lead a military force back to the cave. According to him, there were eighteen other men there when he had sneaked away, but, he cautioned us, soldiers were always showing up, staying for a few days, and then leaving. They traveled North and South and used this cave as a staging and rest area. He also warned us that he had been told an entire Regiment was due to pass through the valley at any time.

There was little danger of his desertion being realized, because he told a few of the other soldiers who were stationed there that he was going back home – back to North Viet Nam.

I asked Gem why he hadn't just gone back home instead of coming to us and was told that he had no family left there and the South Vietnamese government was offering him money to be a Chu Hoa. He basically said he had nothing better to do and if we would give him money, he would use it to support himself for a while until he found a job in Saigon. So, in this case, the program worked.

The problem of the size of the force worried the Major, who was the ranking U.S. officer in the compound at the time. And, it certainly worried me. If we took a large force we would probably be heard or spotted before we got close enough to do any good, and if the force was not large enough it could easily be ambushed and wiped out in that jungle. A small force in VC Valley was an invitation for disaster.

We finally agreed that, all things considered, a surprise attack at night, by a small force, would probably be the most efficient and effective means of achieving the most success.

This force would have to leave our compound under the cover of darkness, find the cave, attack it, then quickly withdraw completely out of the valley and back to a secure area, for there was no telling how large of an enemy force would or could be mustered by the VC and NVA in the valley. If the attacking group was pinned down in the valley they would have little chance of getting out alive.

My PRU were the perfect force for such a mission, but we were not after VCI, so technically I would be violating the CIA's orders by using them in such a manner. I talked it over with the Major and Be and I suggested that we use some of the PRU and some of Be's bodyguards, and thus it would not be a true, PRU operation. They agreed, but when I asked, "When do we leave?" the major exploded. He had no intention of letting any American go on the operation, much less someone in my position.

Yes, he was a Major, and he was the ranking American commander in the compound. However, I was not directly under his command. I ran my own operations separate from his orders or interference. But, he would receive real heat from Saigon if something happened to me on an operation that was not technically related to my true job function, and he had let me do it.

A few months after I arrived in Viet Nam, the PHOENIX Program was becoming a hot item politically, and PHOENIX advisors were high on the VC list of priorities. They wanted a prisoner whom they could force to tell the world about the program and Saigon wanted to make sure none of us obliged them. We were to send the PRU, but not accompany them on any more missions.

Basically I had been ignoring the order. Again I was no hero, but I was not going to send men out on missions that I did not deem safe enough for me to go on. These were my missions. I did most of the work preparing them and I wanted to make sure they were handled correctly. Besides, I was not going to sit inside a compound for a year, I would go crazy with boredom. So, I continued to do what I had done since getting to Tuy An.

The Major really didn't care, because I was making him look good. Our successes were being praised in Saigon, and so American military big shots and American political big wigs had begun to come to the district. If there is success anywhere, these people gather to try to soak up a little of the glory for themselves. Although the Major had nothing to do with the program, and didn't really know exactly what I did, he managed to be in the limelight when the big brass came and it had to help his career, so he let me do as I wanted, as long as I continued to be successful at it.

He finally relented, unhappily, when I reminded him that an American would have to be on the ground if we needed to call in air support, and that this was too dangerous a mission not to have that back up. He did, however, order me to stay back and not participate in the actual raid.

My interpreter, Gem, unfortunately was in Tuy Hoa because of a medical problem and thus I was to be without an interpreter. I did not feel that I could order Barnes or Clack to go on what was basically a Vietnamese operation, so Be offered to have one of his bodyguards carry my radio with direct communication with him. The Major was to stay in Be's bunker and monitor the Vietnamese frequency in case I had to call for air support to get us out of trouble.

I explained to Hung that I was going along only as an observer and to be able to give him quick air support. I told him that he was in total control of the operation and I could tell he was relieved about that. We left the compound after dark and moved directly into the jungle.

The first two hours were spent at a slow trot down familiar trails, with three men well ahead of us to scout for booby traps and ambushes. This was a relatively safe area, so we were able to use the trails to get us on our way. Then, as we began to enter the thicker jungle the going got much slower. We could not use trails if we wanted to avoid being ambushed and in a jungle it is impossible to walk in a straight line. By the time you circle trees, cut your way through vines and bushes, and wade swampy areas, hours pass and you have not traveled very far.

As it got later and later, the jungle continued to get thicker, and the light filtering in from the moon decreased considerably. We were traveling so slowly that I finally placed my hand on the back of the soldier in front of me. I have no idea how Hung and the Chu Hoa found their way, but we wound around and through the jungle growth until 3 am.

Finally we stopped completely and a PRU appeared next to me and motioned for me to watch our back trail. I couldn't see three feet, but did as he indicated. I figured that anyone coming up behind us couldn't see anything either, so the darkness was definitely my friend in this area.

Then the Chu Hoa appeared with Hung behind him. Hung pointed to my M16 and then to the Chu Hoa and told me, through his motions, that I was to kill the man if he tried to get away, or if we were ambushed. The logic was simple, this could all be an elaborate trap and if it was, then the Chu Hoa was going to be the first one to die from it.

I nodded that I understood.

Hung hesitated for a moment as if trying to decide whether I would kill the man. He evidently decided that I would, smiled, and walked away.

To say that I participated in the attack would be a lie. I simply sat, waited, and tried to see what was going on. The silence and darkness were hard to bear. Several times I thought l heard someone talking, but was never sure.

After an hour of this, my nerves were on edge and the Chu Hoa looked as apprehensive as l felt. He alternately stared at me and then at the M16 which was pointed at him. He gave me a couple of feeble smiles, but he was not happy about the situation, and I could not relax for fear that he would escape.

I am sure that by now he was definitely having second thoughts about his decision to defect. The money would be nice for him to have, but only if he was alive to enjoy it, and he must have been feeling that the chances of that were getting slimmer and slimmer.

While he was considering his fate, I was wondering if I could just shoot him if anything went wrong. Shooting someone who is shooting at you is one thing, but shooting someone who is standing defenseless in front of you is something else entirely. Besides, how would I know if it was his fault, should a firefight erupt? Anything could happen, considering where we were, and it probably wouldn't be because of him.

But, Hung told me to shoot him if anything went wrong. Did I want to cross Hung out in the middle of a jungle, especially considering I had no idea where I was? Did I want to cross Hung at any time for that matter?

Finally, I made the guy sit in front of me and I tied his hands behind him with the small rope he wore around his waist. If anything happened, I decided that I would keep him with me and try to get him back to our compound. His fate would be decided there, based on what we found out had happened. I was not going to simply shoot him. I took out my Buck knife and held it up to his face so that he knew I had it out and ready if he tried anything, and then settled back to wait.

It's really difficult to remember exactly what went through my mind as I sat there in the darkness. I know my mind started to wander a few times, but I could not let it. I did not want to let any sudden noise or movement catch me off guard, and I alternated my gaze from the Chu Hoa to the direction from which we had come, to the direction Hung had gone.

However, looking back down the trail was like trying to look through a black wall. No matter how hard I squinted I couldn't see more than three feet in any direction. Finally I bent over to pick up a small twig to chew on and the Chu Hoa jumped. I assume he thought I was bending over to stab him. When he saw what I was doing he again gave me a weak, pathetic smile.

I started wondering about this guy. If the mission was a success, what kind of a life was he going to have? He had made his decision to defect, but no one likes someone who has betrayed his friends.

This guy was in for a very rough life, regardless of the outcome of this operation.

Suddenly, just north of me, the jungle erupted into light and thunder. Then, much to my surprise, except for the noise of jungle animals, all became quiet again. After a few more minutes small arms fire broke out and then just as suddenly ceased. A few minutes after that, another explosion ripped the silence. Then small arms fire broke out in earnest and 1 recognized some of the sounds as being AK47's, and I did not think that they were ours.

Hung materialized next to me grinning from ear to ear. He said "Number One - Boo Co VC". Then he looked at the way I had the Cho Hoa, grinned even more, patted me on the back, and said, "DiDiMow."

Basically he was telling me "We did a great job and killed a lot of VC, but now we have to get the hell out of here!"

Our retreat was much quicker and louder than our entrance. We were more worried about what size of a force might be behind us than we were about what might be in front of us. So, rather than stop and set up a perimeter we radioed Be that we were going to be coming all the way back to the compound. He alerted his security elements and they were waiting to let us in through the wire and mines that surround the perimeter at night. This was a dangerous procedure and one which Be usually forbid. No commander in his right mind would put Be to this much trouble unless he had good enough news to sway Be's bad humor.

But, by the time we finally got there it was already daylight, so there was no problem getting back into the compound anyway.

Hung obviously had tremendously good news and although I had been there, 1 didn't even know what had happened. We entered the compound and were met by Be and the Major. Most of the troops disappeared into their quarters, but before they left, they all, each and every one of them, came up to me and patted me on the back and grinned. Then Hung indicated that I was to accompany him into Be's apartment.

We were met with tea on the table and Hung began his story. I certainly hoped it was a good one, because Be had that veiled look in his eyes that 1 knew could be deadly. The Major kept looking at me and I could tell he had a million questions, but luckily with Hung talking and one of Be's men trying to interpret, he didn't dare talk to me.

I listened to the interpretation of Hung's story with as much apprehension as did the Major. It seems that the Chu Hoa had led the point man of our group to within 50 yards of the cave before he realized he was that close. Any sound by any of us would have probably meant our deaths. After leaving the rest of us so he could stealthily check out the situation, Hung crawled to within 10 yards of the cave, where a small campfire, set back under a ledge, allowed him to see all that he needed.

Two sentries were on duty, one on top of the cave and the other one under the ledge, near the fire. Hung took quite a while to maneuver to where he could kill the one on top of the cave with a knife, then quickly and quietly killed the one near the fire by simply jumping down on him from above and using the knife before the man could yell out.

Then, since he did not know what was inside the cave or how deep it went, he simply crawled inside. Hung was the soldier that all of the Rambo type movies try to emulate, but he was for real.

It was pitch dark inside and he crawled right over a man who was asleep just back of the entrance. The man awoke and angrily asked what was going on. Hung muttered something about having to take a leak. The man cursed at him and went back to sleep. Hung crawled on inside and since he couldn't see anything decided he would leave a small explosive where he was, crawl back outside and set it off. He killed the sleeping man on the way out and once outside set off the explosive charge.

Thus, the light and thunder I heard.

The PRU then waited a few minutes for the dust to die down, then advanced to the cave. A few VC were managing to crawl out and they were immediately shot. The cave opening was partially blown closed, but Hung and a few men managed to get inside with flashlights. They found twelve dead VC in the front chamber, and a large store house of goods in the back section of the cave. We could not carry away all the supplies and they couldn't be left for the VC in the area, so Hung set off another charge to temporarily seal the entrance.

About then more VC who were in the area, but had not been in the cave showed up and began to fire at us. That's when Hung came to me and we quickly left the area.

Hung continued to tell Be about all the supplies that were in the Cave and more details of the operation, but I dismissed myself to the Major and went to bed.

A few hours later I awoke to a bee hive of activity. Be had already sent an army of troops into the area to recover the supplies. The Major was in the air flying air cover with a squad of choppers, and the entire compound buzzed with talk of our operation.

Within three days our compound was overrun by powerful people, both American and Vietnamese. Hung was a celebrity and to be given the United States Army Bronze Star during a ceremony in our compound. He was also to be given several Vietnamese awards. All of the other Vietnamese who had been on the operation were also to receive awards.

The Major pulled me aside and explained that since I was a PHOE-NIX advisor, and as such was not supposed to even be out on missions of this sort, he could not possibly recommend me for a medal. If he did, he would be admitting that he allowed me to go. As far as the Army was concerned, I had never been out of the compound.

This was fine with me. I promised my wife before I left the states that I would not get any medals, and besides, I had done absolutely nothing to earn one. Sitting in the dark, watching a Chu Hoa, and being scared to death is not an adequate recommendation for a medal.

However, evidently Hung had included me in all of his reports because from then on I was looked upon as a hero by the Vietnamese in Tuy An. I eventually did receive a Bronze Star from the Army, but it was for running the most successful DIOCC in all of Viet Nam, and it was certainly not for any conspicuous bravery on my part.

THE UNITED STATES OF AMERICA

TO ALL WHO SHALL SEE THESE PRESENTS, GREETING:

THIS IS TO CERTIFY THAT
THE PRESIDENT OF THE UNITED STATES OF AMERICA
AUTHORIZED BY EXECUTIVE ORDER, 24 AUGUST 1962
HAS AWARDED

THE BRONZE STAR MEDAL

TO

FIRST LIEUTENANT RICHARD C. WIEBURG, 05715078, INFANTRY, UNITED STATES ARMY

FOR

MERITORIOUS ACHIEVEMENT
IN GROUND OPERATIONS AGAINST HOSTILE FORCES
IN THE REPUBLIC OF VIETNAM FROM JUNE 1968 TO APRIL 1969
GIVEN UNDER MY HAND IN THE CITY OF WASHINGTON
THIS 13th DAY OF MAY 1969

CREIGHTON W. ABRAMS
General, United States Army

Stanley R. Resor
SECRETARY OF THE ARMY

54

UNITED STATES MILITARY ASSISTANCE COMMAND

By direction of the President

THE BRONZE STAR MEDAL

is presented to

FIRST LIEUTENANT RICHARD C. WIEBURG

United States Army

For distinguishing himself by meritorious service in connection with military operations against a hostile force during the period June 1968 to April 1969 while serving as United States Liaison Officer and PHOENIX Representative, District Intelligence and Operations and Coordinating Center, Tuy An District, Phu Yen Province, Republic of Vietnam. A competent advisor with practical experience and driving determination, Lieutenant WIEBURG vastly improved the intelligence activities in his area of responsibility. He was instrumental in the establishment of a detailed intelligence base which contributed greatly to the denial of areas of operation and bases of supply for the Viet Cong Infrastructure and inflicted numerous losses on their ranks. Exhibiting sound judgement, versatility and stamina under conditions of stress and hardship, he contributed immeasurably to the effectiveness of allied intelligence operations in the Republic of Vietnam. First Lieutenant WIEBURG's performance of duty was in keeping with the highest traditions of the United States Army and reflects great credit upon himself and the military service.

Chapter 7
A WOMAN PRISONER

Dai Uy Be had an ingenuous, if somewhat twisted mind. He always seemed to get his way, regardless of the situation. If he could not get what he wanted from one prisoner, then he might eliminate that man and get the needed information from the next.

However, I remember one instance where his more conventional means simply did not work and he really had to dig deep into his bag of tricks to achieve the desired result.

One afternoon as Sgt. Clack and I were playing catch with a football in the compound, we saw a squad of Be's bodyguards bring a woman into the compound. Something in their manner was different and I couldn't figure out what it was at first. Clack and I watched for a few moments before I realized what was weird. The woman was obviously a prisoner, and was obviously thought to be a VC, but Be's bodyguards, who were usually terribly brutal, were being very careful with this woman.

They were almost being cordial to her. This really puzzled me.

She was taken into Be's interrogation bunker and just as I began to walk over, Be came out of his chambers and told me, by a shake of his head, that I was to stay away.

I located Gem and found out that the woman was suspected by Be of giving or selling information to the VC. This was a very simple explanation, but something in Gem's manner made me think there was more to the story than he was willing to tell me.

More than half of my job in dealing with informants hinged on my being able to detect lies and half-truths, and I definitely felt that I was not getting the whole story.

I got the girl's name from him and then went into my DIOCC and searched my informant reports for any mention of her name. When I found nothing there, I went through my alphabetical list of known and suspected enemy agents working in my district. Again I found nothing.

I had begun to go through my descriptions of agents for whom I had no name when a commotion arose outside.

I walked outside and found that the girl was being carried, not dragged, to the flagpole in the center of the compound. She was placed next to the pole and made to squat with her back firmly against it. She was tied to the pole in such a way that she couldn't stand up, sit down, or move anything but her head. The entire weight of her body rested on her bent toes. The pain, after a very few minutes would have been horrible. A blindfold was added to top off this new form of solitary confinement.

This form of public punishment was entirely new and 1 felt there must be an explanation of some sort forthcoming. As I have said, it was Be's district and he generally did as he felt best, but he was held account-able by his superiors in Saigon, and he knew that I would have to send in a report through Clarkson, and he knew that there were certain things which Clarkson would not ignore. This was sure to bring about some sort of recriminations and Be was generally a little more discreet.

I quickly wrote, and had translated, a formal written protest to Be. In it I personally assured him that I could not overlook this form of in-timidation and that I would have to send a notification to my superiors in Tuy Hoa. I asked him to please give me some sort of explanation so that I could try to help him stay out of trouble.

He was still standing outside of his house, so I walked over to him with the note, handed it to him, and then told him basically what it said.

I tried cajoling him. I said, "Come on Dai Uy, you know I can't ignore this. You can't publicly torture someone. Take her inside so she is out of my sight."

He offered me nothing in the way of an explanation or apology. He just continued to smile and said I should do what I thought I had to do.

He left me, walked over to the girl, and began to speak to her very softly. I could not make out anything he said to her but whatever it was it did not make her any happier. She tried to spit on him and I was afraid she had sealed her own fate. I waited for him to pull one of his pearl handled pistols and finish her.

Instead he simply got up and walked away, brushing the dust off of his usually immaculate, heavily starched fatigues. As he walked up to me I tried again.

"Dai Uy, she's just a girl. Take her inside, out of the sun, and I will forget the whole thing. Neither one of us wants the hassles this is going to bring us. She can't be worth all that trouble."

He looked at me very seriously and said, "I know what you have to do, and I know what I have to do." Then he quoted McArthur, "People grow old only by deserting their ideals".

"Crud, Dai Uy, you are going to make me grow old quickly if you keep doing things like this." "Besides", I said, "you know that McArthur was relieved of his command and you and I are too young to just fade away."

He thought about it, trying to translate what I had said into Vietnamese, then when he got it all, he started laughing, patted me on the shoulder, and walked into his house.

During the two days she squatted there I never saw anyone take her food or drink, but Gem insisted that she was given water at varying intervals. I do know that she was not taken away so that she could see to her bodily functions. I had to leave my DIOCC the following day because of the smell of her excrement.

I had sent the message to Clarkson and got back a reply that I was just to wait and see what happened and then let him know. He reiterated that I was not to interfere, and I was not to send a report through regular Army channels. I didn't need to be told any of that. Be might like me and he might laugh at my humor, which a lot of people didn't, but he would not hesitate to try to have me killed if I blatantly tried to overrule him in his own District.

On the second day, I walked over to Be's apartment and again voiced my displeasure at his inhumane treatment of the "prisoner".

He sighed, said that again I did not understand his people or their ways, and then waived a hand to one of his guards. The guard walked out of the doorway and headed toward the girl. He untied her and with the aid of a couple of other men, slowly helped her to straighten her legs. She screamed pitifully. They then carried her to Be's underground bunker.

I did not know it at the time, but this was all part one of Be's plan. I suppose that he had actually been waiting for me to come to him and again complain about the treatment of the girl.

Several hours later a squad of soldiers left the compound and headed to Phu Tan, the small hamlet only a couple of kilometers away. They returned near nightfall with five prisoners. All five of them had been severely beaten and they were all taken to a number of cells near Be's bunker.

These cells were not generally used because they looked out over the compound and Be did not like for prisoners to have a view of anything.

I recognized a couple of them and with Gem's help, found out who the others were. I had them all in my files, but couldn't figure out why they had been arrested. I knew that they were VC sympathizers, but they were harmless, they were basically just farmers. If they had been worth the trouble I would have had them picked up long ago. They were sympathetic to the VC cause, but had never done anything that would have warranted Be's attention. Picking them up and treating them in such a manner made no sense, but then again, nothing in the last two days had made sense, to me. As I was to find out, it made perfect sense to Be.

The next morning the woman was brought out. She had been cleaned up and wore new clothes. She had to be helped along, as her legs were understandably still cramped, swollen, and her toes might never be the same. But, otherwise she did not look too bad. Be had his arm around her as he helped her hobble to the front gate. Once there, he gave her a large sum of money and tried to send her on her way. She tried to re-fuse the money and seemed very upset, but Be made an elaborate show of placing it in her hand. Finally she left with it, but she was issuing a string of un-pleasantries at Be as she did so.

As l turned to go about my business I noticed that Be's five prisoners had been watching the show, and the method to Be's madness finally hit me.

Later that same day the prisoners were beaten, warned to stop work-ing to help the VC and then released.

A week later, while going thru my informant reports from the pre-vious night, I came across the girl's name. It seemed that she had been killed, murdered, mutilated in fact, by the VC. A note was supposedly found wired to her tongue, stating that this was an example of what would happen to anyone who turned against their friends and gave or "sold" information to the Imperialist backed South Vietnamese forces.

I knew that Be had probably already heard the news, but I showed him the report anyway.

He had obviously gotten a kick out of his elaborate frame, so I asked him why he had gone to so much trouble, why he hadn't just killed her himself.

He looked at me as if l were crazy and then replied, "She was my brother's wife. She was, how do you say it? Oh, my sister-in-law. I couldn't kill her! My family would not forgive me for that!"

What a way to fight a war!

The woman prisoner tied to the flagpole.
My DIOCC is in the background.

Chapter 8

HUNG

Trung Se Hung played such an important role during my life in, and return from, Viet Nam, that I feel I must devote at least one chapter to him.

He was an extremely complex individual and I have never tried to judge him or even try to give reasons for, or credence to, his actions. All I can do is relate what he did and how he reacted under different situations. He could be as kind as, and as cruel as, anyone I have ever known. His love for the South Vietnamese people was only exceeded by his hatred for the Viet Cong and the North Vietnamese. You are free to judge him, to determine whether he was right or wrong in his actions, and to decide whether he was morally correct or a totally immoral person. I have just tried to present the facts as I saw them.

I will relate two separate incidents that occurred involving him that may give you a further insight into the man and help you in your decisions regarding him.

I was having breakfast one morning when I was summoned by Dai Uy Be. I forgot my dried eggs and went immediately to his office. He told me that one of his companies had surprised a small group of VC on a trail near Phu Duc Hamlet. Two of the VC had been killed, but one young man had lived, although he was seriously injured and was going to have to be immediately taken to Tuy Hoa.

I said, "Ok, Dai Uy, was this guy a VCI?" I was wondering why Be was telling me this if he wasn't.

Be said that he didn't think the guy was, but he was letting me know because he might need my help with the prisoner later on. Then he offered me tea and changed the subject so obviously that I knew I shouldn't bring the guy up again.

When I got back to my DIOCC, I went thru my files and checked with my informants, but I could not find anything that indicated this man was any more than just an average VC foot soldier. The name I had been given wasn't in any of my files of known VCI so I was not interested in him, and wondered why Be had bothered me with him. Actually I wondered why he had bothered to go to the trouble of taking the guy to Tuy Hoa at all. Usually he would have just listed three VC as killed in action.

A few days later, however, Be again sent for me and asked if I would go to the Tuy Hoa Air Force Base Hospital and interrogate the prisoner that he had sent there. Be had received information through his grapevine that the man might be more valuable that we had at first thought, and might even be able to give us the whereabouts of a sapper squad that had been giving us a lot of trouble. (Sapper squads, or "dac cong" were specially trained independent groups of Viet Cong soldiers whose job it was to hinder the movements of our troops.)

Even if he could give us the information, he was still not a VCI and I wasn't supposed to waste my time on mere soldiers. But, I had been looking for a chance to get into Tuy Hoa, so I told Dai Uy I would be glad to and would leave at once.

His casual, "Please take Trung Se Hung with you," made me stop in my tracks.

I said, "Dal Uy, the man is in an Air Force hospital. Hung can't do anything in there, and I don't need any trouble with the Air Force. I better just take Gem."

Be was adamant. "Please, you take Hung also. I talk to him. He be no trouble."

I could tell that Be was going to insist, so I thought I might as well agree right away and save myself a lot of grief. Besides, Hung was smart enough to know that he couldn't do anything "inhumane" in a United States Air Force Base. At least I hoped he was.

I enjoyed the ride to Tuy Hoa, and Hung, through Gem, talked a lot more than was usual for him. He told me some of his life. He had been through some sort of Jungle School training given by the CIA, had been trained in hand to hand combat, and had even been, according to him, on a few LRP (Long Range Patrols) with the Green Berets. I began to wonder if he really spoke no English, as he led us all to believe.

When we arrived at the base I had no trouble locating our prisoner or getting permission to talk to him with Gem. Getting Hung allowed in the room took a little longer. We were all three finally allowed in, after we left all of our weapons outside in a locked container. I simply put down my M-16 and my Buck knife. Gem only had an M14, but it took Hung a couple of minutes to shed all of his weapons. I knew he carried a couple of pistols, along with his AK 47, but I had no idea he had so many knives on him. He had seven of them hidden around his upper body and legs and it was obvious that although they could not be seen, they were all easily, and readily accessible to him.

The head nurse watched us put everything in the cabinet, and then she made it pretty plain that she not trust Hung at all and was certainly going to keep an eye on him. Finally, she escorted us into a large room. It was obvious that she was determined to stay behind Hung.

I say room, but it was just a long metal, barracks type building with cots along the walls on both sides. There were about ten bunks per side and all were filled with prisoners. It looked like a scene from MASH, with everything white and sterile looking and smelling of rubbing alcohol. There was an MP at each end of the room and all the windows had bars.

Be was right. The man had been seriously injured. He had obviously been pretty well shot up, and probably beat up after that. Most of his face was in a cast and I assumed his jaw, or jaws had been broken. One arm was in a cast and both legs were in traction. A large metal pin pierced the skin of each leg, passed thru each knee and came out the other side. The ends of each pin were attached to cables which went up and over a bar at the foot of the bed. The cables hung down the other side of the bar and were attached to a large cement weight that hovered just above the floor.

I've seen the same sort of arrangement in hospitals in the States and always thought it was a very barbaric looking arrangement. Who wants to lie in bed and see a pin going thru his own knee, and worse, to have that knee pulled high in the air and held there with cables and weights?

Anyway, the man was obviously in a lot of pain, although he had a morphine drip going. He was sedated, and with all the damage and repairs that had been done to his face, he was really hard to understand when he talked. I asked the questions and Gem translated. The man swore that he was not a VC, but had only been walking down a trail with a few friends and had been ambushed. Sure, we all believed him!

I tried being nice and I tried being angry but I was obviously not going to get any information from the guy. He played the innocent routine to the hilt and if I had not heard it a thousand times before I might have believed him. The guy was a VC, but I became convinced that he was nothing more than a poor misguided foot soldier. He wasn't a VCI and I shouldn't be wasting my time on him. The PHOENIX program guidelines were very explicit and this guy did not fall under any categories that I was supposed to be investigating.

When Hung came up behind me and asked, thru Gem, if he could talk to the guy, I was very apprehensive. I stood right next to him for 15 minutes while they talked back and forth in a very civil fashion.

Finally, since Gem grew tired of interpreting their casual conversation and walked away, and thus I had no idea what they were saying and since Hung was obviously going to be nice to the guy, I wandered down the aisle and struck up a conversation with a nurse who was on duty.

I was having a nice chat with her when all of a sudden a terrified expression came over her face. She tried to speak, but no words came out. Instead she pointed past me to where our prisoner lay.

I whirled to see Hung, standing at the foot of the man's bed with both hands raised above his head, with the cement weight tightly clutched between them. He was calmly asking the prisoner questions, and the prisoner was desperately trying to answer.

The MP that I could see had pulled his 45 and was yelling at Hung. I'm sure the one behind me was doing the same thing. However, neither could shoot Hung because if they did he would drop the weight, and then everyone would be in serious trouble. And of course the prisoner would have no leg.

The next few moments were pure bedlam. All of the prisoner's in the ward began yelling at Hung, the head nurse appeared from behind a curtain and began screaming at me, the nurse I had been talking to turned white and froze, and I ran toward Hung. Before I got to him, he lowered the weight, smiled at me and walked over to where Gem was looking out of the window and pretending not to notice that anything was going on.

One MP grabbed Hung and we were all "ushered" out of the room.

For a couple of minutes I felt for sure that the MP's were going to shoot all three of us. They might have actually done so, but we were all unarmed, I was an officer, and they would have had to do a lot of paperwork.

It took all of my diplomatic powers of persuasion and every bit of personality I could muster to keep them from throwing us directly into the stockade. I really think the MP's were so stunned that they were not sure what to do. I quietly explained that Hung was a mental case and that I would get him out of their area immediately. Besides I said, if this goes any further, you two will be in trouble for letting it happen.

They were still undecided, so I told them it was all just a sick joke by Hung, and I said, "Guys, you have to admit it was kind of funny." They said a lot of things and none of them were very nice, but they finally let us go, and as we left I saw them talking and starting to laugh.

By the time we reached our jeep and were on the road out of there, I had recovered sufficiently to ask Hung what the hell he thought he was doing.

He just grinned and muttered something. Gem translated: "He found out what Dai Uy Be wanted to know".

Gem started laughing and after a few minutes I had to pull the jeep off to the side of the road. I was laughing so hard, partially from the absurdity of the situation and partially from released tension that I couldn't drive.

On the way back, I asked Hung if he would have actually dropped the weight, thus jerking the man's leg completely off, if the poor guy hadn't given the right answers.

Hung laughed and said, "Oh, yes. For sure. Number 1."

Can you imagine what the Army and Air Force would have done to me? I can, and it is not a pretty thought. Needless to say, I never took Hung to another Air Force Base. I did, however, go on many more "operations" with him, and one of them in particular more clearly shows another side of the man.

I had been getting scattered reports for weeks that there was a VC unit operating from a small island just off the coast. I hadn't paid too much attention to the reports as I was very busy in another area, until one day the name Bui Danh appeared on a report. He was worth my paying attention to. Mr. Bui Danh was the VCI equivalent of a town mayor or hamlet chief and he was very good at his job. He had been, according to my reports, spending a lot of time in the hamlet of Phu Tan, spreading propaganda, helping collect taxes and recruiting soldiers. I had not been able to pin down any of his movements and this was the first report that might help me "set him up".

My job did not involve going after or tracking, on paper or other-wise, small VC bands. I was only interested in this particular group if Bui Danh was indeed staying with them. So, I put a little extra money out to my informants, but told them I expected more information on this one individual.

Within three days I had five separate reports involving him; three of which indicated that he was spending the day light hours on the small island, only a short distance from my headquarters. It was really not an island, as it was actually connected to the mainland by a long narrow sand bar.

I went to Dai Uy Be with the information and asked his permission to "borrow" a few of the villager's fishing boats for an overnight ambush. He gave me very little encouragement, which was a pretty good sign that the information was no good, but he told me to do whatever I thought I needed to do.

We left the compound at 2200 hours and commandeered eight small canoe-like fishing boats. I sat in the middle of one with Gem in front and Hung in the rear. Barnes was in another canoe with the radio and two other PRU members. There was very little moon so we felt comparatively safe paddling across toward the island. When we reached it Hung sent the canoes back with strict instructions to the owners that they were not to mention our going to anyone.

We trekked inland a few hundred yards to a small knoll and there set up a protective perimeter. From our position we could overlook most of the small island once it became light, so we settled down and waited for Bui Dan and his bodyguards to return from their mission.

As always I simply curled up in some bushes with my camouflage blanket and went to sleep. Hung was in charge of posting guards and seeing that the watches were changed. The mosquitoes were not at all bad on the island so I had a decent couple of hours sleep.

I set my mental alarm to awake me just before BMNT (Before Morning Nautical Twilight) and it went off on schedule. I very quietly got into position for the ambush. But, after watching for two hours after dawn, it became evident that no one was going to walk into our trap. We decided to search the island in case they had been there all the time. By 10:00 we were hot and tired. There had been no sign of anyone having been on the island for quite some time.

I gave the Vietnamese copies of the reports with the informant Code names on them to Hung and told him to look them up and have a little talk with them. They were taking the CIA's money but delivering false information, and I wanted it stopped.

Hung knew that I didn't like excessive "pressure" being applied to the locals and by the expression on his face I knew that he was a little confused as to what he was to do. I told Gem to explain very carefully that I wanted the informants punished and an example made of them, but I that I did not want them killed, or even seriously hurt.

Hung gave me a disgusted look and walked off.

To him I'm sure I sounded indecisive and perhaps a little soft. I knew I had better watch my step and give him no further cause to doubt me. His logic was simple and I understood it perfectly: The informants had lied to us, therefore they were working for the VC. Therefore, Hung should be told to kill them. If I kept him from killing VC, then my loyalties were in doubt. The last thing I wanted was for Hung to doubt me, so I had to watch my next steps very carefully.

By noon we were ready to start back, but since the boats would not return until dark, Hung decided we would go fishing. He did not, however, bother to tell Barnes or me. He pulled the pin on a hand grenade and then threw the grenade into the ocean inlet that separated the island from the mainland. Then he motioned for me to follow him and walked about 40 yards down the beach while the rest of the PRU made quick poncho shelters to protect themselves from the sun.

Barnes asked me what was going on, but all I could give him was a shrug of my shoulders as I walked down to where Hung was waiting for me. I was still pondering our last conversation and began wondering if maybe this was going to be some sort of confrontation. In the middle of these deliberations three more grenades were thrown into the inlet by the PRU.

Hung laughed when I jumped at the sound of the first one. Then, removing his boots, pants, and shirt, he motioned me to follow suit and he dove into the water. If Gem had been around I would have been asking a lot of questions, but since he had been left almost a mile behind as part of a rear guard, I really had little choice but to follow.

We swam about 50 yards out into the water, then Hung disappeared under the surface. When he reappeared almost a minute later, he had a large fish in each hand and was grinning from ear to ear. He nodded down and evidently wanted me to dive.

I was still a little confused, but did as he indicated. At first I couldn't see anything, but as my eyes became accustomed to the water and as I dove deeper, I saw enough to truly amaze me. The ocean floor was covered with fish, which had apparently been dazed by the concussion of the grenades. I was beginning to run out of air, but had always been proud of my ability to hold my breath a long time underwater and was not about to let Hung outdo me in this. I managed to pick up a large fish in each hand and kicked for the surface.

The PRU on the bank cheered when I broke water with the two fish. The tension which had surrounded the entire group for the last few hours was broken and the following hours were some of the most enjoyable, and memorable, of all my time in Viet Nam.

How Hung knew exactly where the fish would be lying, or why the fish were on the bottom, I have never figured out. Any dead fish I had ever seen, floated on the top of the water. Hung and I dove until we were both thoroughly exhausted. Other PRU members and Barnes took turns swimming out to us and carrying the fish back to shore. When I could not tread water or dive any longer, I swam back to shore and fell exhausted, but happy, on the hot sand. Hung did likewise.

After resting, I walked back up the beach to where the grenades had been thrown in, swam out and dove in that area. There were no fish on the bottom in that area or any other place that I could find.

The boats arrived and we again paddled back to the mainland. It was after eight at night when we arrived at the docks. It was O.K. to leave our compound after dark, but getting back in after dark was very difficult and quite dangerous. I assumed we would move to an area where we could set up a perimeter and wait out the night. Instead, we walked into a cluster of huts in the dock area of the hamlet.

Hung led the way, rousing villagers from their beds as we walked through their huts. These were fishermen and evidently they went to bed early so they could get up before first light. In the center of this cluster was an open area and there we all stopped. Hung gave a few orders and several of the PRU's retreated in various directions -perimeter security I assumed. Then he ushered me into a hut and pointed to a straw mat where a few seconds earlier a girl had been lying. She had jumped up when we entered, bowed, and then left the way we had come in. I started to argue but immediately sensed that it would be impolite and decided to satisfy him by lying down for a few minutes.

71

That few minutes turned out to be a couple of hours, and would have been much longer had I not been awakened. During my sleep the villagers had evidently been busy, for when I emerged from the hut, there, where the clearing had been, was a large table overflowing with food.

Small torches were burning around the area, illuminating a scene I will never forget.

The low table was at least fifteen feet long, and down each side sat many of the PRU and many old men whom I assumed to be the village elders and political leaders. Women and children were standing around the table and everyone seemed to be waiting on me. Hung was at one end of the table and motioned for me to sit at the one empty place at the opposite end.

The feast we had that night is hard for me to describe. I have eaten at the best restaurants in many parts of the U.S., at outdoor barbecues, at a Luau in Hawaii, and fine restaurants in Japan, Saigon, Mexico, and Latin and South America, but never have I had better food, or had more pleasant company.

Gem had arrived while I slept and had been seated so that he would be on my right. He explained that as I was the honored guest, everyone would wait for me to begin. If I liked the food I was to please smile and nod.

I smiled and nodded for two hours and even today I still find it hard to talk about that evening without getting misty eyed. Those people who had so little, and who could look on me as an intruder, an interloper, an outsider, treated me as the prodigal son and bestowed upon me more honor and dignity than 1 truly deserved. I began to understand why Hung hated the VC and loved these people.

I, like most Americans, had generally considered them to be one and the same - they are, and yet they are not. And that was what Hung had at been trying to get across to me for months. I have no idea what became of Hung after the Communists took over the country. He could not have stayed there. He would surely have been killed. Maybe he made it to the states and is living here, but his love was with his people in South Vietnam, so I cannot conceive of his being truly happy elsewhere.

*These are the fish we picked up off the bottom of the ocean.
I am the one on the far left. The other three are PRU.*

Chapter 9
WANTED POSTERS

As the number of VCI eliminated in Tuy An District began to increase, so did Saigon's interest in my District. By the time I had been there for three months we were getting more VCI per month than any other district in Viet Nam. We stayed at the top of that list for the remainder of the time I was there. The reason for this was because of two people; Be and Hung. It had little to do with me. They were absolutely the best at their respective jobs.

After a few months of this success, we began to have visitors come to the District. At first they were unimportant; just Lieutenants, Captains, and Majors from other Districts and DIOCC's who wanted to know why our district's program was so much more effective and more successful than their own.

Then a General arrived and his motives were entirely personal. He wanted publicity and our program was a hot item. It seems that the entire PHOENIX Program had been leaked to the press and everyone wanted to know about it. My wife sent me a copy of a magazine that contained an article about us. It referred specifically to the PRU and called them the "Butchers of Viet Nam".

A little later, two very high ranking men in our government arrived. The first one was a real pain in the rear. He came with a chip on his shoulder and was, like the General, looking for publicity. I was never adverse to talking in front of a group, and I liked the limelight that such dignitaries brought. So, I really put on a show for them, their aids, and their bodyguards.

I had charts showing exactly how many VCI had been eliminated at three different levels: hamlet, district, and province. I had files on each individual who had been neutralized (captured) or killed, his previous jobs/activities, his contacts, his position with the VCI, and the details of my DIOCC's work in locating, identifying, and eliminating the man.

As I said, the first politician had a chip on his shoulder and started out by trying to contradict my numbers. He felt that they were inflated and/or fabricated. Basically, he was calling me a liar and insulting my intelligence, my integrity, and my honesty. I found this to be a little irritating.

I kept my cool and read some of the actual firsthand accounts of a few of the ambushes. Then, I brought Hung and a few of the other PRU in and let them explain, through Gem, a couple of our recent action reports. There was no way that anyone in their right mind would consider contradicting Hung to his face, but the man made it obvious that he did not believe him. The man finally just said that he was going to take a few of my files so that he could review them and discuss them with others in Washington.

As politely as I could I told him that would not be possible.

I had been thoroughly indoctrinated in the PHOENIX program and those weeks in the underground passages in Saigon had impressed upon me one thing. I was never to release any of my files to anyone who was not directly connected with the program. The "fat man" (as Gem referred to him later) and his Colonel were on a tour. They had no authority over me, other than the obvious fact that I was only a Lieutenant and the gentleman accompanying the politician was a full bird Colonel.

The Colonel looked at me like I was crazy and told me I would do whatever the man told me and if that was not sufficient that he himself, as a Colonel would give me a direct order to do so. He reminded me that refusal to obey a direct order in times of war could get me court martialed and could get me hung. Of course he used the age old questions, "Do you know who this is? Do you know who I am? Do you know who you are talking to?" (I know that is poor English, but that is what he said.)

Then he proceeded to act like I was not even present any more and began to apologize on my behalf, to the "fat man". I just stood back out of the way and tried to figure how I was going to get out of this one.

Evidently the Colonel thought that I had lost my mind and that his verbal abuse would be sufficient to stop any further interference from me. I must admit that I was scared. I was not, and still am not, the hero type. I had never disobeyed an order in my life, and would never have considered ever doing so. Hawkeye Pierce would think me extremely dull.

It would be nice to say that I stuck by my guns and physically threw them both out of my DIOCC. But, that did not happen. I got lucky and was able to avoid a direct confrontation because Dai Uy Be came by at precisely that moment and took them into his office for tea.

I immediately went to the radio room and called my direct superior, Clarkson, in Tuy Hoa. He backed me up completely. He said that I was to lock up my files and under no circumstances was I to release any of them, or sign anything, even if it meant defying a direct order from the Colonel. This was very easy for him to say as he was a civilian and he was a long ways away. He could not face court martial and I certainly could.

I locked up the files, locked the door to the DIOCC, wrote a message to the Colonel that he was to radio Clarkson as soon as possible, and then took my jeep and drove out of the compound. I drove to a restaurant in Tuy An. I figured that if the Colonel could not find me to give me a direct order, then I could not be hung for disobeying what I did not receive. (Cowardly or Smart? Probably both, because it worked, but it was not a brave thing to do.)

When the Colonel's aid appeared an hour later and asked for the files and for me, Gem gave him the message. Gem also told him that I had been called away due to an emergency involving my PRU.

According to Gem, the Colonel was not happy, but he made the call to Clarkson. After that call he was so mad he would have probably shot me had I been around. Eventually, he regained his composure and he and the "fat man" left our compound without getting anything else.

Clarkson later told me that I would have been in serious trouble if I had released any of the files. I asked what he meant by serious, and he replied that the Colonel's threat of a court martial would have been the least of my worries. He said that the CIA was to be feared way more than was the Army. He added that the Army was at least still civilized.

It has been over 44 years since that incident and the PHOENIX Program is certainly no longer Confidential, so I hope I am still not under any such restrictions.

Hung was extremely upset by the fact that the man had been questioning our successes and what he had been insinuating about our operations. Hung took it very personally, and I can't say that I blamed him. The guy had basically been calling the PRU and me, liars. Hung kept asking me, through Gem of course, what he was supposed to get as proof. He asked if he was supposed to have the PRU bring all of the bodies of the people that were killed during ambushes all the way back to the compound?

I told him of course not. That would not be safe, practical, and was certainly not necessary. I have said many times that most of the ambushes occurred at night in the middle of the jungle. If we were in relatively safe areas, we would sometimes quickly check the ambush area, grab what paperwork we could, check all the bodies and then quickly withdraw to prearranged sites and set up perimeter security. In the morning, if we felt we could do it in relative safety we would go back to the site and check it out in daylight.

In areas that were not safe enough to check out immediately, we relied on reports from villagers, or we got a larger group of soldiers, or the entire PRU squad and went back to the area as soon as we could. The reports from villagers were very reliable, and if anything were conservative and certainly not exaggerated as to results. Whether we were immediately able to see the bodies or not, there was no way I could have PRU ambush cells of four men try to carry back bodies of dead VC.

So, we went about our business and I just tried to forget about everything the man had said and implied. A few nights later, I had the PRU in four different ambush locations in the district, with four men in each position. I took the other four PRU and we set up our own ambush at another location.

My group had no luck and returned to the compound at daybreak. I was immediately told that Hung's group and one of the others had been very successful, but had not yet made it back. I hoped that Hung would come back in a little better mood after getting some VC, and that some of them were the VCI we had actually been after in the individual ambushes.

An hour later the different cells began returning. However, none of them reported immediately to me in the DIOCC, which was normal procedure. On the mornings after ambushes, although I had been up all night, I always waited in the DIOCC until each group returned so I could find out how they had done and to make sure that all of them were all right. Each group always came right to me because they knew I would be waiting and anxious.

This morning however, none of them came. After another hour I sent Gem to see what was going on. He came back immediately and said that they were all waiting for Hung to return. They had never done this before and I asked Gem why they were doing so. He said he didn't know, but I knew immediately that he was lying.

I let the lie stand, and continued to wait without questioning Gem any further. I figured he had his reason for lying to me.

Thirty minutes later I was told that Hung had returned and would be with me in a minute but first he was meeting with the other PRU's. Sure enough, just a few minutes later all the PRU came in together. Hung was carrying a paper bag which he promptly handed to me. He told Gem to tell me that it was the proof of the kills they had that night. I was very hesitant to open the bag but figured I had to.

Sure enough, the bag contained a large number of ears. Hung said that if people wanted proof of the kills each night, then he would deliver them proof. Later I found that Hung had told the leader of each cell

79

that if they got any kills that night they were to cut off one ear from each man. When they got back, the other cell that had been successful gave their ears to Hung. The bag contained the "proof" from each group.

Besides the ears, Hung gave me a large number of papers, which proved later that one of the casualties had been one of the VCI we had been after. I guess one of those ears had been his.

I had to be very careful with how I handled this. Obviously I could not let it continue. I did not want the title, "butchers of Viet Nam" attributed specifically to my group. But, Hung had actually only been doing what the idiot from Washington asked him to do. He was bringing in proof. Hung was definitely not the type of individual I could yell at and criticize in front of the other troops, or even privately for that matter. So, I had a problem.

I had found the best way for me to handle a big problem was to do nothing rash on the spur of the moment. It was always best for me to wait, let things cool down, and give myself time to think things through.

I congratulated Hung and the rest of the PRU for a very successful night and then told them to go take showers and get some sleep. I asked Gem to have Hung come and see me later in the afternoon, after we had all had some rest.

Late that afternoon, I was back in the DIOCC when Gem and Hung came in looking very apprehensive. I started by again congratulating Hung for the success he had had that night. Then I asked him if he agreed with my estimation that the guy from Washington was an idiot.

He said, "yes, for sure, he number 10" and then he spat, like he was spitting on the guy. (#1 was extremely good, #10 was the worst thing Hung could say in English about anyone.)

I said, "So Hung, do you think we should ignore everything that guy said."

He said, "He ngu ngoc, (a rough English translation would be Stupid, Dumb Ass, etc.) we do nothing he say."

"He wanted us to bring in proof of every kill we have. Do you think we have to go to the trouble of doing that Hung, just for that ngu ngoc?" I asked.

Hung hesitated, looked at me for several seconds, realized the problem, and then turned to Gem. According to Gem he said, "I do not do this for that mother." (That is not the translation I was given, but it will do) " I bring back the proof for my friend Trung Uy, so that he know I not lie." (He was referring to me, as Trung Uy is Lieutenant in Vietnamese)

I took a step toward Hung and actually hugged him for a split second. I had never seen that done in Vietnam, and in fact, I had never seen anyone even touch Hung in the time I had been there, but I took a chance. I stepped back and said to Gem, "Tell Hung that he never has to prove anything to me. I trust him with my life every time we walk out of this compound and I know that he would never lie to me, just like I would never lie to him."

Hung stared at me for a second, and then he bowed lower than I had ever seen him bow. Usually he just nodded his head. Then he turned and left. Gem was looking at me with a mystified expression and I wasn't sure how this had worked out, but I had a feeling I had done the right thing. Finally Gem smiled and said, "You good Joe".

I gave him the bag and told him to bury it. I did not want anyone making a necklace out of them as I had seen the Montagnard (Mountain Yards) do. I had three Montagnards in the PRU and knew that given the chance, it was very likely that they would do so.

I never received any more ears and we never talked of proof again, although, I noticed that from that day on, I got more proof that I had ever received before. It came in the form of more captured papers, more written eyewitness accounts from members of the PRU, and many more confirmations from villagers.

I would hate to think what Hung would have done if I had tried to punish him in some way for that one night of indiscretion. I'm sure I would not have made it out of Vietnam alive if I had done so.

The second "political big wig" was a different story. He arrived a few weeks after the first, and I liked him immediately. He listened to my presentation without interrupting and then asked a few intelligent questions. He treated Hung with the utmost dignity and respect, and made a big point of complementing him and the rest of the PRU on the fine job they had been doing in support of the United States effort in the war. When I was finished he and his group began to file out of the DIOCC for the traditional tea with Be. As he walked past me he handed me an envelope and said he would like to talk to me later.

The letter inside the envelope was from Clarkson. In simple terms it said I was to "talk straight" with this man. l was to answer all of his questions as honestly as I could, but I was still not to release any files or sign anything. He also suggested that if there was anything I wanted, that this man had a lot of political clout and could probably get it for me.

The man came to the DIOCC by himself an hour later and told me he had heard a lot about my work and our successes in the District. I started my usual spiel about how great Hung and Be were, but he stopped me and said that he understood everything they were doing and that he also understood how tremendously hard it must be to work with such individuals. He was very complimentary of my actions and "buttered" me up pretty good. It was great to get such complements, but after all, he was a big time politician. His job was to soft soap people, so I took it with a grain of salt.

Then he asked if there was anywhere we could get away from everyone and talk a little more privately. I called Hung and Gem and the four of us piled into my jeep, leaving his bodyguards, drivers, and aides just staring after us. I drove to a "restaurant" in Phu Tan. Hung and Gem sat at an outside table while the man and I sat at another one further inside.

Of course he was at first very apprehensive about being out in Viet Nam without the bodyguards who had always been with him, but I assured him that Hung was worth more than all the men he had left in our compound and that the food was completely safe. He played it like a true politician and although I'm sure he still had his doubts, he kept smiling.

We had a very nice lunch of some sort of brazed meat. He started to ask what the meat was, but I could see him think better of it, shake his head and continue eating. I definitely liked this guy.

After an hour of my fielding his very intelligent questions in regards to our operation, he gave me the opening I had been waiting for. He thanked me for being so open and honest with him and then asked if there was anything he could do for me.

Ever since Clarkson told me this guy was coming and that he might be able to help me with anything I could come up with, I had been thinking. I had gone to college in Arizona and had raced horses in Ruidoso, New Mexico, and Oklahoma, so I was very familiar with the tales of the old west. When I was in Lincoln, New Mexico, I had seen old Wanted Posters on Billy the Kid and other famous outlaws and wondered why some sort of wanted posters couldn't be used in my situation. After all, I was after "outlaws" and I had their names and descriptions.

So, I asked the man if he would help me produce and finance Wanted Posters on the VCI in my district. This was certainly not what he had in mind, but as I explained he became interested and then got really excited by the idea. He said he could understand how we had become so successful if I had been thinking out of the box like this in regard to our ambushes and other ventures.

I suggested that we offer monetary rewards ranging from high to low, depending on the rank and/or importance of each individual. I had no idea where the money would come from (I guessed the CIA), or how the posters would be printed. I suppose I originally had some vague notion of my drawing them up by hand.

Anyway, he said he would personally take the idea to Saigon and probably to Washington where he would present it to the higher ups in the PHOENIX program and see if he could get things rolling.

When he finally got ready to leave, I had no idea if I would ever hear from him again, and I certainly had my doubts as to whether the Wanted Posters would become a reality. But, what the heck, I certainly had nothing to lose.

As a last minute statement, I said:

"You keep telling me what a great job my men and I have been doing, but did you know that we are having this success while using the old, antiquated weapons the Army has issued us. Most of my men are using World War II, M1 carbines and we are fighting soldiers using modern Soviet and Chinese weaponry. We are really operating at a distinct disadvantage here. The only modern weapon we have is my M16. We even rob the people we kill of their AK47's, and ammo for the captured weapons is obviously a problem. I am a United States Lieutenant and the leader of a mercenary squad, run by the CIA, and my men have to rob the VC to get modern weapons. What sense does that make? Just think what we could do if all of my PRU had new M16's. Just something else for you to think about!."

He looked at me seriously and said, "No Vietnamese units have been issued M'16's. Those are just for American troops."

I told him that I knew that, but asked him to think what a big deal it could be for him, if he was the first politician to authorize their being issued to our "brothers in arms".

He laughed and said Clarkson had warned him to be careful with me and now he knew what the man had meant. He said that if he had known me better he wouldn't have left himself so wide open. He also said that I was much too truthful and open to be a politician but that if he could help me in any way after the war, I should get in touch with him.

As it turned out, he outdid me to no end - which is probably why I was only a Lieutenant and he was a senior member of our government. Before he left I had given him a list of the people I wanted on the posters, their rank in the VCI organization, and any descriptions that I had available on these people.

A few weeks later I received two large bundles. Inside were about 20,000 Wanted Posters. The fact that I actually received these fantastic posters amazed me, but the truly staggering part was the amount of money offered for the apprehension of the VCI that I had listed.

To give you an idea of the amounts, the average Vietnamese earned about 50 piasters a week. (Piaster was the name of the Vietnamese currency in use at the time.) The reward for the lowest man on my list would have been over a year's pay for a Vietnamese. I don't remember the exact amounts now, but as I recall, the reward for the top man was over 100,000 piasters.

The posters were delivered by helicopter with orders that the pilot was at my disposal. He flew me all over the district, while I threw out handfuls of the posters every few seconds, littering the jungles and hamlets on a large scale.

I had been up in choppers constantly since arriving in Nam, but this guy darted in and out, up and down, and made me as sick as a dog. By the time I threw out the last of the posters I just wanted back on the ground.

I would certainly love to tell you how wonderful this program turned out, and that I had "bounty hunters" coming in constantly with these men and asking to collect their rewards. That's what I had imagined would happen, but unfortunately it did not happen that way.

I've often wondered why it didn't work any better than it did. I really thought I would have VCI being turned in left and right. I had envisioned that they would be tied up and brought in by villagers, or that the villagers would come in and give me information as to their location. This would have also led to their being paid if the information panned out. The money offered had to be a temptation to many destitute Vietnamese, but very few rewards were actually collected.

Remember that I had already been paying informants throughout the District and I paid them good CIA money every month. However, they were clandestine operatives and they guarded their identity very closely. If one of them started supplying me with bad information, I had to have Hung go straighten them out. He was one of the very few people who knew all of them by sight.

Perhaps I did not have a practical means for villagers to provide me with the information needed to satisfy the Wanted Posters without endangering their own lives. Or maybe there were other, "cultural" reasons. Whatever the reasons, the lack of success of this program has always alluded me, but it could lie somewhere in the ideology of the Vietnamese people. They are people who will steal and consider it OK as long as what they steal is for their family. They will fight for what they believe in and give up their own lives if necessary. But, for some reason they would not turn in the people on my list, although I got informant reports on the same people weekly. It was weird.

A couple of funny things did happen as a result of my posters. Shortly after I threw the posters out of the chopper our compound was shelled one night with satchel charges. Their outside coverings were interesting to say the least. The VC had wrapped my posters around powder and bits of metal and had fired the charges into the compound where they were supposed to explode. They were very ineffective "bombs", but a few people were injured. Several of these charges did not explode and thus we found the very "unusual" use of my posters when we took them apart. They actually tried to use my posters to get back at me.

Several weeks after this, Hung came into the DIOCC and said he had a Wanted Poster for me. I said, "so what"? Then I found that he wasn't talking about our posters. He was talking about a handmade poster the VC had made and put my name on.

Of course it also had Be's, Hung's, and a few other PRU's name on it, but I was at the top of the list. Quite a compliment! That one poster is the only one I ever saw and it was confiscated by Be. He was probably mad because my name was above his and I never saw the poster again. I would love to have it now. I mean, how many people get their name on a wanted poster - other than bad guys, of course.

I thought that was the end of my involvement with the "Washington Man", but, a few weeks later Clarkson called and told me he would be in Tuy An in an hour and that I was to have all of my PRU there at the landing pad.

I had no idea why he was coming and he didn't say. He never ventured out of his tightly secured compound in Tuy Hoa, so I knew I was either in real trouble or something very important was going on. As I said, he never left his compound, in fact during the year I knew him, this was to be the first, and only time I saw him out of it. If he were ever captured, it would be an unimaginable political catastrophe for the U.S. He was a civilian and he was basically running the PHOENIX program under the auspices of the CIA. The North Vietnamese and VC could have done all kinds of things with him.

His chopper, and a couple of others, including a gun ship, landed a couple of hours later and on them were crates of M16 rifles and thousands of rounds of ammo. He even sent a few hundred rounds of AK47 ammo. It seems my friend from Washington had come through again. Clarkson said that these were the first M16's ever issued to anyone other than US soldiers.

This was quite an event and Clarkson had brought along a news team to take pictures and film what was happening. Somewhere in the U.S. a few nights later, I'm sure I must have been on the 6:00 news.

I have some black and white pictures of us handing out the weapons, but cannot publish them because of the people pictured in them.

Man, does it pay to make friends with the right people?

Chapter 10
TRUNG SE DOC

Every man must, if he is to be happy, find his niche in life. He must find a place where he is loved, wanted, and probably most importantly, needed. Most people are under the erroneous impression that prisons are terrible because they serve poor food, have cold beds, dish out hard work, and allow so little freedom. But, in all of those areas, men in prison are probably better off than most of the people on the outside. The real torture of being in prison, or so it seems to me, is being forced to be in an environment where you are unloved, unwanted, and not needed.

John Grimes, or Trung Se Doc as he was called in Tuy An, had found life in the U.S. to be like living in a prison. He had been through two unhappy marriages; his children despised him and his ex-wives used, but hated him. He could not hold a job as a civilian and he was constantly getting into trouble and being demoted by the Army. He was a total failure, both in the eyes of the world and more importantly, in his own eyes. That is, until he was transferred to Viet Nam, and ended up in Tuy An.

He arrived as a forty year old corporal, two years before I came on the scene, and during those two years he unlocked the doors of his own prison. He found for the first time in his life, his niche. He became loved and needed.

The small hamlet of Phu Tan had no doctor, nor did any of the hamlets that made up the district of Tuy An. Dai Uy Be originally had a doctor in his compound who was supposed to administer to the sick and wounded of the district. However, this man was so uncaring and under qualified that John, who was only a corpsman, almost immediately became the man Be called in cases of emergency. By the time I arrived he was lovingly known as the "mayor of Phu Tan". He was not treated as a corpsman; he was treated like he was a full blown medical doctor. No foreigner in all of Phu Yen Province was more respected than was Trung Se Doc.

I was happy in the states. I had a beautiful wife, a university degree, a teaching certificate and a career in front of me. I was to serve a one year hitch in Viet Nam, and then was to be sent home. Doc had just signed up for his third consecutive tour in country. One man's prison can be another man's Shangri-La.

By the time I had been in the country for six months, Doc and I had become fast friends. He gave me an old Russian made rifle which had been presented to him, and he kept inviting me to go to Tuy Hoa and spend the night in a house that he was renting there. It seems he had acquired this house, complete with "maids" that he assured me were both pretty and safe.

I kept turning Doc down, as I was married and believed in the sanctity of that relationship. However, my replacement arrived and he quickly took Doc up on any and all invitations.

The Army had pulled another of its typical maneuvers. While I arrived in country a day after the man 1 was replacing had left, my replacement arrived six months before I was due to leave. His name was Lt. Vick, and he was as green, or greener, than I had been. He was a nice enough guy, but he didn't really care to do much work. He was constantly trying to get out of the compound with Doc or anyone else to avoid the hours of paperwork that the DIOCC required.

On one particular Friday after he had been in country for a few weeks, I had had enough of his excuses and stalling tactics. I looked out the door of the DIOCC, where I had been working on files for two hours, and saw Vick in a jeep with Doc, heading out of the compound. I walked out and asked where they were going.

"Oh, in to Tuy Hoa to help Doc. We'll be back early Sunday. I was going to ask you, but Doc was in a hurry and I knew you wouldn't mind", came Vick's reply.

There were several things about his answer that really bugged me, or else I would have probably just waved him on with a grunt of disgust at his lack of any kind of a work ethic.

First, he was not going to help Doc with anything. He was going to get "laid" by Doc's girls. Second, Doc never came back from Tuy Hoa until Monday. Third, Doc was never in a hurry and would have strongly suggested that Vick check with me first. Fourth, Vick knew that I would mind for a lot of reasons, but mainly because l was particularly worried about the part of Highway 1 over which they would be traveling.

I had been receiving scattered reports for days indicating that it was being heavily mined by the VC. I had suggested that all U.S. personnel travel by Chopper for a while. At least, until I could check out the reports, get more concrete evidence as to what to expect, and try to get the Army to check the area and remove any mines that might be there.

For the first time since his arrival l told Vick, NO! He got out of the jeep and walked over to the DIOCC, grumbling under his breath. I tried one final time to talk Doc out of driving. "You can live without those girls for another few weeks. Besides, Doc, you can get anything you want or really need in Phu Tan."

He knew what I was hinting at and that I was truly concerned for his safety.

"Lieutenant, there ain't no need for you to worry. l been traveling that road for nearly three years and no little kid with a mine is going to stop me from seeing Ma Sung. Why don't you come with me? Vick won't mind. You been doing his work since he got here. Besides, those girls will make you forget about all that 'shit' paper your always frettin over. You can forget the ambushes for a few days."

"Can't Doc. I've got one set for tonight and l will have to supervise this one personally. But, if you have to drive in, watch the roads. These reports are from usually reliable bugs."

"Shoot," was all he said as he drove off.

Vick took my refusal fairly well. I had enough paper work to keep him busy all afternoon, and I took him out on his first ambush that night. Then, on Saturday morning I put him to work going over our latest informant reports.

That afternoon I took him to my favorite "restaurant" in Phu Tan. I put restaurant in quotes because I don't want you to get the idea it was like any eating establishment in the States. A restaurant in Phu Tan was simply a few sheets of tin, plywood, or cardboard nailed to a couple of posts, forming a sort of lean-to that kept the occupants relatively dry and out of the direct sun. Inside were two tables with wooden benches for chairs, and a curtain for a partition that separated the eating, sleeping and cooking areas.

Vick had not eaten out of the compound since his arrival and was understandably apprehensive. He kept looking around, I suppose searching for hidden VC. He asked me three times if I was sure that the food was safe to eat. I kept reassuring him that we were as safe as we could be in Viet Nam, and told him to relax and enjoy the fact that we were in a beautiful country, the sun was shining, and that the food would be great.

Then he started asking me questions about the food. What would we be eating? Was the meat really going to be dog? Had the vegetables been properly washed? How would we know what was in the soup?

There was one thing I learned quickly in Viet Nam, and that was you never asked what was in the food. I ate everything served to me, never worrying about what was in it, and I was usually pleased with the taste. If it tasted good and I knew it was not poisoned, then why worry about anything else. I am probably the least curious person in the world, so I learned to just eat and enjoy.

I have been asked several times what the menu was like. What were the main entrees, etc? I can honestly say I never saw a menu. You just sat down and they served you what they had cooked for that day. There were no choices.

Hung had taken me to all of the spots he felt were safe for me to eat, and had introduced me as his friend. So, I kept to those places, kept my

M16 next to me, kept a careful watch on everyone walking by, and kept any questions in regard to the food to myself.

Vick was too curious, too nervous, and too new in country to enjoy the moment. He kept trying to figure out what was in the soup, especially the round, soft objects that "popped" when he bit into them. I asked him if he liked it and he said that he did.

"Then why worry about what it is. Just eat it and smile and nod to that young lady. She wants to know if you are pleased. Besides, if you play your cards right you might get an after dinner treat. If you want it that is."

Hung had once told me that I could get anything I wanted in this restaurant, and had evidently told the old owners to try to please me. They always did just that, and had their very attractive daughter serve me. Hung knew that I was faithful to my wife, and I believe he respected that decision, but it did not stop him from teasing me about the fact that the daughter could be part of the "menu" if I so desired.

Vick was single, however, and was definitely interested, and the girl seemed intrigued with him.

"Ah, you're kidding me. She's not that kind. Is she"?

"What kind is that kind, Vick? She's got to help the family make a living and between the Americans and the VC, she doesn't have too many choices."

Finally, to satisfy his curiosity on both accounts, he motioned the girl over and tried to ask her what was in the soup. She smiled and tried to understand, but obviously didn't. Finally she went behind the petition and brought out the old, lychee nut chewing, owner's wife.

This old crone smiled, bowed and said, "You like, yes?"

"Oh, number one," smiled Vick.

"You with Hung's friend. You welcome. You want nookie?"

The lychee nut juice rolled down her chin and she showed us her black teeth in a huge smile.

Vick was embarrassed, but tried again. "This. What's in this?" he said pointing to the soup and ignoring her question.

"That octopus soup. 1 make. Good. Make you strong in bed."

"But what are these?" Vick insisted, fishing one of the round objects out of the soup. The realization hit him even before the old woman grinned and said:

"Eyes!"

He jumped up and barely made it out of the opening before he began to throw up.

The old woman and I howled with laughter, but the young girl frowned at us and followed Vick outside. She brought him back inside and ushered him to the back, where one section of the lean to served as a bedroom.

I finished my meal of some kind of barbecued, what I assumed was pork, and was outside, sitting against a wall, letting the sun soak into my fatigues when Vick emerged. He had a smirk on his face and was blushing terribly. I don't know if the blush was because of the incident with the food or the girl.

We went back to the compound after first stopping off to examine and take pictures of a bridge which had been blown by the VC a few days earlier. Saigon wanted a complete report and 1 felt pictures would expedite my explanations and save me a lot of work. When we arrived at the bridge, Major Lee was there and we took a few pictures of each other next to it.

Our first report of Doc's trouble came at about noon on Monday. A radio message came in stating that a Marine convoy traveling north from Tuy Hoa on Highway 1, had been ambushed. I went to Dai Uy Be to see if he had the same report. As usual, he had the more accurate news. The convoy had had several mines detonated under a couple of their trucks, and although there was a little small arms fire, probably from the one VC who had been left behind to detonate the mines, they were definitely not under attack.

Our next report was from Doc himself. He had come upon the convoy and was aiding a couple of slightly wounded Marines until the Medevac chopper arrived.

I told him to take care, and he laughed.

"Hell Lieutenant, there are more Marines here than there was at Iwo Jima!"

I signed off with a request that he send someone to look for and try to capture the guy who had detonated the mine. I stressed the fact that I wanted him alive.

Doc said it was too late for that. The marines had caught him hiding in a rice paddy east of the road, and he was now incapable of talking.

The next message came by way of Be's grapevine. The message was that Doc had been blown up by a mine. I tried to reach someone at the scene, but Doc was the only one there on our frequency, and he wasn't answering. Finally word came from a chopper pilot that someone from our compound would need to come to the Tuy Hoa hospital to identify the body of the soldier that he was taking there. It was not a Marine.

To say that l was distressed, upset, or mad would not adequately describe my feelings. I simply had a sick, queasy feeling in the pit of my stomach, and I felt weak and helpless. There were all kinds of conflicting emotions and feelings clashing in my head. There had to be something I could do. I asked Be if his reports definitely indicated that it was Doc.

He said he had asked several times and a couple of people from Tuy An had actually seen Doc after the mine exploded. They assured Be that it was Doc.

I had to do something so I started to get in my jeep and drive to the scene, and then on to Tuy Hoa, but the Major walked out and reminded me that I had only a few months left in country and that I would not accomplish anything by getting myself blown up. He said he would call me a chopper. It made sense. The chopper would get me to the hospital much faster than the jeep and would certainly be a lot safer. However, sitting in the compound and waiting for the chopper nearly drove me crazy.

We got the full report a few hours later, just before the chopper arrived to take me to the hospital.

It seems that Doc and the Marine medics finally got the wounded taken care of and the Marine column continued up Highway One. Doc did not immediately leave. There was an old deserted temple near the spot where they had all stopped and Doc got curious. He stepped off the road and was looking around the remaining ruins. There are many such in Viet Nam as the country has one of the longest continuous histories in the world with archeologists finding remnants of human settlements over a half million years old and a cultural history of over 20,000 years. In the last 1000 years alone, the Vietnamese have fought and been ruled by the Songs, Mongol Yuans, Chams, Mings, Dutch, Manchus, and French. So, ruins are numerous and it is certainly interesting to try to figure which rulers had each of them built.

As Doc walked around this deserted temple he got careless and stepped on an anti-personnel mine. That was it. No gun fire. No blazing battle. One unattended mine, one false step, and a "bouncing Betty" ended Docs life on this earth: or so we thought.

When I reached the hospital in Tuy Hoa, l found that he had not been killed after all. He was alive, and the surgeons at the hospital were performing emergency surgery. If he survived these, then he would immediately be flown to Tokyo for further surgery. If he survived those, he would be flown to Walter Reed for more. I was told that it was going to be very close and that he was in extremely critical condition.

A doctor came out and told me it had to be a miracle that he hadn't been instantly killed. The doctor suggested I go get a drink, something to eat, some sleep, and come back in the morning. He said it would be many hours before they would know anything else.

I did what he suggested and when I went to the hospital the next morning I found that because of the severity of his injuries they had risked moving him and had already flown him to Tokyo. He was still alive but had lost one leg and one arm. I was told he would probably lose the other arm and at least one eye during surgery in Tokyo.

There was nothing for me to do but go back to Tuy An and start packing up all of his personal possessions.

A few days later word came that he had survived surgery in Tokyo, and was being flown to Walter Reed Army Hospital in the states. He would still have to undergo further surgery, but the chances were now good that he would actually survive.

I helped pack all his gear and said a silent prayer to ask God to give him the will and strength to find what happiness he could. He deserved more than he had ever received. Maybe he would find God and eternal blessings in heaven. He had found little happiness or peace on earth.

There was absolutely nothing I could do, so I gave up trying to rationalize, feel sorry for, or even think about him. As I had done many times before and would do many times in the future, I simply refused to admit to myself that anything had happened. I crossed him off my mind as if he had never existed.

Doc will reappear only when I become depressed or in a meditative frame of mind. His face will flash across my consciousness and I will quickly get busy with something else. Sometimes it does not do any good to dwell on things over which one has no control.

I'm sure the Post Traumatic Stress Disorder of most Viet Nam veterans today comes from the same sort of behavior. They get flashbacks which they are no longer able to suppress. I have been fortunate. I have very little sympathy for the pains of others. My wife says I am the most unsympathetic person she has ever known. I refuse to go to hospitals, funerals, and even weddings if I can help it. It is definitely a flaw in my character, but it did help me to remain "sane" in an insane war, and to look at it now objectively while others are going crazy.

I had been back in the states for about two months when I received a letter from Vick. He was trying to find a job by mail and had filled out several forms trying to get into the management trainee program with Sears. He knew I had worked my way through college working for them, and wanted me to write him a letter of recommendation. At the end of his letter he said: "We got a letter from Doc the other day. He still has one eye and seems to be in good spirits, considering. He asked specifically that you be given his address and really wants you to write him.

I wrote Vick his letter of recommendation and I started at least ten letters to Doc, whose address was Walter Reed Hospital. However, I never did finish or mail any of them. What could I write? How are you? How's it going? I finally realized that it would be better for me if I just forgot about trying to write the letter, and forgot about Doc.

Would it be better for my friend, Doc? Again I shy away from and don't think about such questions. I could probably not deal with the answers.

97

Chapter 11
LETTERS FROM HOME AND ADDITIONAL INCOME FOR BE

Joeline has always been a wonderful, supportive wife, and she certainly did everything she could to support me during the year I was in Nam. She continually sent me packages of things I liked that were designed to boost my spirit and the spirits of the guys in the compound with me. Some of the items she sent proved to be very helpful, some arrived fresh and delicious, but, the time it took them to get there and the distance involved certainly took a toll on some of them..

The first batch of chocolate chip cookies she sent came in a paper box. They arrived as chocolate chip cookie crumbs, but we still ate every bit of them. From then on I asked her to send all cookies in a tin can. This kept them from getting crushed and also kept them fresh. They were the hit of the compound every time they arrived and everyone there looked forward to my getting the next batch.

Once, she sent a loaf of banana nut bread - at least that was what she said it was. From looking, all I could tell was that it seemed to be alive. It arrived as a huge green mold that reminded me of the old movie, *The Blob*.

In one package she sent three tomato plants. They did well, and I was really looking forward to eating the little red tomatoes as soon as they got a little bigger. However, one night I set them on a ledge in my room and that night the rats had a feast. By morning there was nothing left but the small pots and fertilizer spread all over the floor.

It's amazing how much mail call was looked forward to each day. You might watch an old war movie and see the GI's lining up for their mail - grown men screaming with excitement over a letter or package, or moaning with disappointment when they didn't receive one – and you might feel that the emotions were exaggerated for the camera. Believe me, they are not. Mail from home is the single most important event in a soldier's day-to-day life. It is much more important than food or alcohol or anything else.

Writing letters to someone who is out of your environment, and especially receiving letters from the outside world is a tremendous physiological way to keep you "grounded". They remind you that there is another life out there waiting for you and they give you, in my opinion, one of the most important things in the world - hope.

Of course many of the things I was doing were considered Confidential at that time, and I could not write about them. But, that did not keep me from writing about the people I dealt with every day and describing the country and the everyday life of the soldiers there.

I was lucky! My wife wrote regularly and sent me packages which I opened like a child on Christmas. Several of the people from the 1st Baptist Church in Dinuba, California, wrote to me, and my mother kept me informed as to what was happening with my father and the rest of the family. I received the local newspaper from my wife's hometown, the *Dinuba Sentinel*, and although I seldom read it when I was home, when it arrived in Viet Nam I read every page of it, including the classified..

Phone calls were a different story. I could not, as they do on the "Mash" episodes, simply pick up the radio and call home. To place a call to the states I had to travel to the nearest "MARS" station, which was at the Tuy Hoa Air Force Base. Once there I had to sign up for a call, then hang around the base for a day or two and wait for my turn and the proper weather conditions. The operators would radio the states and some HAM operator would hopefully pick up the call. He would use the telephone to call the required number, so when I finally did get through, there were at least three other people on the line.

I had to say a few words then say "over". The message was relayed to Joeline, then she said a few words and they were relayed to me. If the weather had been perfect I would have been able to hear her, but as it was, everything we said had to be repeated by someone else. It was a nightmare. We finally signed off, and I never tried to place another call. She did not want me to. It had been a terribly disappointing episode for both of us.

Today, I still do not like to talk on the phone - and it must go back to that one horrible call.

Using a tape recorder and sending tapes back and forth was another way of communicating, and these worked out well. Today we have Skype, and that is fantastic, but back in 1968 the computer had not even been invented.

One day while I was recording a letter to Joeline, a satchel charge exploded in our compound. It happened periodically and we all had prearranged points to which we had to run. My position was in the mortar pit. After checking to make sure no one was injured and confirming that we were not under attack, l went back to the room and returned to my recording. The machine was still running and I didn't think to rewind the tape. When she received the tape and was playing it at home, the explosion was a much more traumatic experience for her than it had been for me.

The explosion, then the few moments of silence while l checked outside, and left the tape running, nearly gave her a heart attack. She said our dog, Liebec, a large white German Shepherd, crawled under the bed and wouldn't come out for quite some time.

Communication was certainly different back then. My son was sent to Iraq with the Army a few years ago and even though he was in a remote outpost, as I had been in Nam, by using his computer he constantly showed Joeline and I around his compound and everything he was doing. We could see him and talk to him almost daily. What a comfort that was to us! I am still amazed at the changes that have taken place between the two wars.

Anyway, shortly after those satchel charges that scared Joeline so much went off in our compound, Be came into my office and asked what information I had on a specific area in the district. He had been receiving complaints from the populace in the area that VC were establishing a base there.

I knew the area in question and confirmed his reports. He asked if I would accompany him on a small operation and I jumped at the chance to get out of the compound during the daylight hours for a change.

We could only get one chopper so the number of personnel was severely limited. The new MACV advisor in the District, a Major, decided he wanted to go along, so we took a radio man, Clack, and headed out to the chopper pad. Be brought five of his bodyguards and we took off.

The area we were going to search lay on the eastern side of a mountain and we flew low to the ground so that the mountain would muffle the sound of the chopper. As we popped over the mountain and swooped down on the area in question we caught five people in the open. Since it was a free fire area, the chopper gunners and the Vietnamese in the door opened fire. I saw three of the VC fall to the ground.

The chopper pilot set us down and we all jumped off and began to sweep through the area where we had seen the VC while the chopper rose to give us air cover. The pilot had hardly become airborne when he radioed to us that he was having engine problems and would have to leave immediately. He said he could not set down to pick us up or he would never get back up. He would call ahead and try to get another chopper to come out and pick us up.

We were left stranded, nine men in VC territory with no air cover. Of those nine, there was a Vietnamese District Chief, a U.S. Army Major, and a PHOENIX advisor. If they could get us, it would be a fantastic catch for the VC.

We broke off contact with the VC we had been pursuing and headed south to the sea. We regrouped just off the beach and plotted the quickest and safest route back to our compound.

Our first obstacles were a series of cliffs that lay between us and our compound. As we climbed up and over one of them, we un-expectantly came upon a VC dispensary. It had been temporarily deserted, but had not been so for long; probably only when we attacked in the chopper, and the VC had to be close by.

I had mixed emotions as the Vietnamese started to quickly destroy all the medicine and cots, etc. This was a dispensary, an aid station for wounded. Yet, although it was the enemies I didn't feel we should destroy their medical supplies. I expressed my view to the Major, but he didn't agree. He said we were there to hurt the enemy in whatever way possible, and destroying their medical supplies was a sure way of hurting them.

After leaving the dispensary we ran into very thick hedgerows that we could not possibly cut through. We had to go around them and this took us even further out of our way.

About that time we got some bad news. We received a radio report from Tuy Hoa that because of a number of reasons, there would be no chopper available to extract us and we were on our own in regard to getting back to our compound. Be could usually get choppers for all kinds of reasons, many of them out of proper military channels, but try as he might, he could not get one this time. The Major tried his luck with people he knew but he had no better luck.

This turned an aggravating situation into a dangerous and extremely uncomfortable one. There was no use getting mad. We had to take action and do it quickly. With the small group we had we certainly could not just set up a perimeter and wait for a chopper the next day. Our presence was definitely known and there were large groups of VC in this area. If word got around that Be and the rest of us were stranded here, there is no telling how many troops would be out looking to take our scalps. We had to get moving and hope for the best.

It was just getting dark as we came upon an old deserted hamlet. One of Be's bodyguards fell into a punji pit and two of the stakes impaled his leg. It took us at least half an hour to get him out and of course then he had to be given tetanus shots and the wounds attended to. Then two of his buddies had to carry him the rest of the way back.

That is the exact intent of the pits. They are not designed to kill. They are designed to injure. If you have one injured soldier then that effectively incapacitates at least two others.

We retraced some of our steps and skirted the rest of the hamlet as it was by then too dark to safely avoid any other traps around that area. We were not in deep jungle and there was an adequate amount of moonlight to see fairly well, but not enough to avoid carefully laid traps.

We send a point man ahead of us and put a man on each flank, and continued our trek back. It was very slow going as we had to stay off of the trails. Getting back alive had a much higher priority than trying to get back quickly. For a while we walked through rice paddies, and then hit jungle. Luckily this was not thick triple canopy stuff and we were able to get through it without too much cutting.

After we had traveled a bit further, the point man waved us down. We had barely concealed ourselves when a squad of VC appeared. There had to be at least 25 of them and we had not had time to adequately set up an ambush. We didn't have any claymores and although I knew Be's bodyguards had to be extremely good, I wasn't sure how the Major would react. I had not seen him in combat and for some reason I had my doubts about trusting my life to him. I hoped that Be would just let these guys pass, but to be ready I raised the M79 Grenade launcher that I had luckily carried with me this time. I aimed toward the back of the group of VC because the M79 shell has to travel 30 meters before it arms itself. I really couldn't see a lot that far away, but I knew there were enemy soldiers there. At least the sound of the M79 would certainly scare the VC if I had to fire it. The sound it made when it fired was unmistakable. It was a loud "Whoomph", and then when the shell exploded, well, explosion is description enough. Everyone knew what damage it could do.

Unfortunately, my first fear was realized when the Major overreacted and began firing before the VC were even near the center of our field of fire. I immediately fired the M79 and then quickly brought my M16 to bear rather than reload the launcher. I only got off a quick burst before the VC disappeared into the brush and light jungle, leaving a number of their men dead on the trail. The same trail that we had taken pains to stay off of.

We had been extremely lucky. Especially since the Major had acted prematurely. The VC must have thought they had run into a large enemy force and ran away, rather than trying to overrun us, which they would have done very easily.

Be and I both looked at the Major with disgust, but he was so excited and babbling so much about what a great job we had done that he did not read the displeasure on our faces. I knew that if I stood there I would lose my cool and say something that might get me in real trouble, so I walked to where I knew the 79 shell had landed.

Be saw where I was going and asked if I would search the dead VC while his men watched the perimeter and he figured out our next move. Now, the VC knew where we were and the only thing saving us was that they did not know how large of a force we had. That, they would find out very shortly, as I had no doubt that they would send scouts back to find and keep track of us.

I found nothing of importance on the first dead guy I came to, but the second man had a canvas sack with him and inside it I found a great deal of money. In fact, there had to be hundreds of thousands of dollars in Piasters (Vietnamese Currency). I took papers off of the man and the money and went to the third body. It was very dark where they had fallen under the trees and I had to feel around to find him. I felt in his pockets, took out some papers, and then ran my hand up his torso to find his shirt pocket. I hit dirt and at first couldn't figure out what was wrong. I tried again and again ran out of body at the waist. Then I realized that the man no longer had an upper body. He had literally been blown in half, probably by the M79. I stood up, backed away, and tripped over something. As I got up I felt what I had tripped over - the upper portion of his body.

I said, "the hell with this," and headed back up the trail. I found Be and the Major only twenty yards away, going over the map with a small covered flashlight. They were deciding the fastest way back to the compound. We discussed setting up a perimeter and spending the night where we were, but decided the group of VC would be getting reinforcements and would come looking for us.

So, we headed off again. Just when I thought we were about out of trouble we ran into a patch of prickly pear. Before I knew it, it was all around me. I heard curses coming from ahead of me and knew I was not the only one enmeshed in it. By the time I got out of the patch I was fairly covered with prickly stickers.

Finally, five and a half hours after leaving the drop site, we reached an area where Be had radioed ahead to have jeeps pick us up and drive us back to the compound.

When I finally got to my room and undressed I had to spend another hour picking the stickers out of myself. Then I was so wound up that I started a letter to Joeline.

The following day I went through the papers I had taken off the dead and found that the guy with the money had been Nguyen Lon, a big finance chief in the district and one of the top VCI on my list of most wanted. One of the others had been a low level VCI on my list. I dropped by Be's quarters and gave him the money and a report on who the men were. He was extremely happy about getting those two VCI, but I think he was happier with the money.

We had been exceedingly fortunate and I quickly sent a full report to Tuy Hoa, but I had a feeling I should leave out all the details concerning the money. I just mentioned the papers that confirmed who the two VCI's were, and let it go at that.

A few days later I received a note from there asking if Mr. Lon had had any money on his person. I went to Be and told him that my superiors in Tuy Hoa wanted to know how much money Lon had on him. All of my reports on him had indicated that he was a big finance chief and everyone knew he carried around large sums of money.

Be smiled and said, "Did you mention any money in your report?"

I told Be that he should know me better than that.

So he said, "What money'? I know nothing of any money. Just papers."

So, rather than lie, I simply ignored the inquiry from Tuy Hoa. They sent the same message a few days later and I ignored it as well. They didn't ask again and I didn't hear any more about it. It had been a very successful night for Be in more ways than one.

Chapter 12
GUNG HO JOE

I have always felt that here are four types of individuals in the work place, whether we are talking about a small business, a large corporation, the teaching field, or the armed forces.

First there is the dead beat. This is the guy or gal who is totally incompetent, lazy, and who gets more demotions than promotions. This is the person who cannot hang on to any kind of a job for any length of time, and whose poor attitude brings everyone around him down to his level of incompetence. A good CEO recognizes and gets rid of these as soon as possible.

Second, there is the average worker. He does his job, tries to perfect his skills, and moves slowly but steadily up the promotional ladder. In this day and age this category probably makes up 90% of the work place. Unfortunately, during Viet Nam, because of the draft, the percentage of soldiers in this category was considerably less.

Of course there is the good employee. This is the guy with intelligence and imagination, who does his work and helps others. We all wish each and every employee fell into this group.

Finally, there is the "Gung Ho Joe". This man is dangerous, both to himself and to anyone around him. He should be avoided at all costs. He is so concerned with making a good impression on his superiors and moving rapidly up the promotional ladder that he will lie, cheat, steals others ideas, stab his co-workers in the back, and in the military he will end up endangering lives in the process.

I met a character in the fourth category while serving my first year of duty in the Army as a Battalion basketball coach in Fort Hood, Texas. This guy always grated on my nerves. He was always looking for ways to impress our superiors, and he did not care who he had to embarrass, criticize, or belittle in doing so. He cared about himself and his career above all else.

When we all received orders for Jungle School and Viet Nam, he began sleeping outside, "to get used to it".

Now, to me, that is just crazy! If I have to undergo hardships, I will do so, get them past me, and then go on to other things in life. But, never would I consider sleeping outside in Texas to get used to sleeping outside in Viet Nam. Why would anyone have to practice at being miserable?

This guy even began to soak his clothes and then walk around in them because he was told that in Nam you were wet a lot of the time. He went so far as to buy cases of "C" rations and refused to eat anything else for the last few weeks we were to be in the states. My wife and I, on the other hand, tried to make my last days in the states enjoyable and we certainly ate as many excellent meals as we could.

Unfortunately this nut went to Panama when I did, then to Viet Nam with me, and even ended up in the PHOENIX program with me.

In Panama he surpassed his stateside idiocy. There we were undergoing weeks of Jungle School in a wretched place that surpassed Viet Nam in heat, bugs, snakes, and as far as the military was concerned, in stupidity.

We were being instructed in the art of jungle survival by a group of Green Berets whom I swear did not have a total IQ of over a single digit. Again, please don't feel that I am condemning the Green Berets as a unit. I'm just saying that those who instructed us in Panama had to be on the lower evolutionary chain of that organization. I suppose they were not fit to be sent to Nam to fight, so the commanders tucked them harmlessly away in the jungles of Panama and hoped they could at least be useful in training new Lieutenants.

A couple of incidents might point out the reasons for my conclusions and give you an even clearer picture of Lt. Green, my Gung Ho Joe.

We were sitting in the grass in the middle of an enclosed area and one of the Berets was telling us about how a soldier must be prepared to eat anything to survive. He had pointed out many edible plants that were also to be found in Viet Nam, and was moving on to edible animal life. He talked about the nutritional value of different jungle insects and animals, and even handed around a platter which contained cooked snake. He insisted that we all try it.

I didn't mind. I can eat just about anything - in fact, the other Americans in Tuy An called me "Garbage Mouth", and it certainly was not because of my vocabulary as I never cuss. It was because I would eat whatever was left on their plates after they were finished.

The talk the sergeant gave was very informative and I paid particular attention to what could be found in the jungle that was edible. This was definitely not a waste of time.

Anyway I tried the snake and with a little salt it would have been fine, even if it was a little tough. All this time, throughout his talk, the Beret had been holding a white, furry rabbit in the crook of his arm. When his right hand was not occupied with other things, he had been petting the rabbit.

Just as I was beginning to think that the Green Berets, who were our instructors, were not as bad as we had been warned that they were, he started talking about the nutritional value of drinking animal's blood. He stopped petting the rabbit, twisted its head off, raised the body above his head, and let some of the blood run into his mouth. I know this sounds incredible, and overly bloody and vulgar. You may think that I am trying to be dramatic. I am not. It was a vulgar scene, but it did happen.

Then the Beret asked if anyone else wanted to try it.

You guessed it, Lt. Green got up, stepped forward, and let the nut pour blood in his mouth. The Army Colonel who was supervising our group that day was very impressed with Green, as Green had hoped he would be, and Green was assigned to lead our Search and Destroy mission that evening.

I suppose there is supposed to be some sort of correlation between gruesome behavior and military leadership ability, but I've never been able to understand it.

Before I go on with my story about Lt. Green, I've got to tell about what happened later that same day to reinforce my earlier estimation of the soldiers giving us our training. This incident did not involve Green, but he was there.

This time we were all gathered together in a large compound. We were seated on bleachers and were listening to lectures on poisonous and nonpoisonous plants and animals which we might encounter in Viet Nam. During the course of the lecture the instructor unbuttoned his shirt and took out a snake. It was about three feet long, and I'm sure of some non-poisonous variety, and had evidently been crawling around inside his shirt all during his lecture. He walked along the front of the bleachers as he talked, holding the snake out in front, and evidently watching the reactions of those seated on the front rows.

When he had crossed the length of the bleachers he went to two of his buddies and told them to bring "that Lieutenant" up front. He pointed to a young lieutenant whom I did not know, but who by his actions was obviously deathly afraid of snakes.

The scene which followed is one I will never forget, and one which I will never forgive myself for letting happen.

The lieutenant said, "What do you want me for?" and it was evident to all of us that he had no intention of going near the snake. The instructor said, "Just come on up here. I'm going to put this snake inside your shirt."

The Lieutenant leaned as far back into the crowd as he could and said, "Not me man. You're not coming near me with that thing."

The two guerillas grabbed the guy and half carried him to the front. They were joined by two more Berets and between the four of them they held the poor guy still while the fifth unbuttoned the guy's shirt, put the snake inside, then re-buttoned his shirt.

They all moved away and left the Lieutenant standing there with his arms out away from his body and the snake clearly moving around inside his shirt. The poor guy was so scared he just stood still and yelled.

How we all, thirty or forty of us, let that bully of an instructor and his four goons do that, I will never know. It would have been so easy to

110

say, "Stop, let him alone!" and once it was said I'm sure everyone else would have backed the voice.

But instead, we just sat there, glad and secure in the knowledge that they had picked someone else. We were safe, so we said nothing and let that poor guy undergo, what was obviously to him, a horrible torture.

Obviously, they were trying to teach a lesson. Of course there are snakes in Viet Nam, and in the middle of an ambush in the jungle you cannot jump up and run away if you see one. You could get yourself and many of your men killed if you did such a foolish thing. However, you are not going to eliminate someone's fear of snakes by putting one inside that person's shirt. My wife is afraid of heights. If four men were to hang her off of a building, would that suddenly cure her phobia? Of course not! Only a total moron would believe such a thing.

But, those were the tactics used on us in Panama, so you might understand why I did not think these particular Green Berets were the pick of the litter.

Before we left Panama one of the guys in our unit ran headfirst into a black palm. I don't know the real name of the tree, but that is what they called it there. It is simply a tree whose trunk is covered in long, sharp, needles. I had never seen anything like it. I suppose it looks like a long thin porcupine standing up. Anyway, we were on a night escape and evasion and he was running, which he should not have been doing, looked back for a second and as he was turning back he ran straight into one of these trees.

The needles break off on contact, so he had literally hundreds of these black things sticking out of his face, his chest, his legs, literally everywhere on the front of his body. I once saw a man thrown by a horse into cholla cactus and that was bad, but the needles of this tree were worse. They had to fly him immediately to the states and I don't know if he ever got to Viet Nam.

It was almost a pleasure to leave the jungles of Panama and head to Viet Nam, where Lt. Green could renew his quest for promotions.

As l stated, he was also assigned to a district in Viet Nam, but I lost track of everyone once I got to Tuy An. I was too busy with my own problems to worry about how everyone else was doing. However, once, on a buying trip to Tuy Hoa I happened to ask Clarkson if he had any news of the guys I came over with.

He relayed a few minor incidents, said they were all jealous of my districts success ratio, and then asked if I knew a Lt. Green.

I said that yes, unfortunately I did.

He told me this story:

Green had not been getting along with his PRU unit. He wanted results at all costs. He was not concerned with their welfare, just the kills they registered. He reminded them that they were mercenaries and that they were expected to behave like mercenaries - whatever that meant. On one of their missions Green had not done enough "homework" on the people he was after and because of his failing to get sufficient intelligence, two of his PRU were killed.

The leader came to Clarkson and asked that they be transferred to another district, or that Green be transferred out of their district. They were mercenaries and were prepared to accept the dangers of their profession, but they would not have any more of their own killed as a result of improperly organized missions. They insisted that the deaths were a result of Green's lack of planning, and not because of any action or lack of action on their parts.

Clarkson asked the man to be a little more patient, but told him he would talk to Green. A few weeks later Green again planned and led an unsuccessful mission. This time he jumped out of a concealed ambush position and attacked a squad of VC on his own. It was, I suppose, a very brave, but an equally stupid act. I guess Green must have wanted to prove something to himself or to the PRU, whom he must have known were not holding him in very high regard. As the VC fled into the jungle, one of the PRU, who had momentarily failed to fire because Green was in the way, caught a random round and was killed.

This time the PRU took matters into their own hands. A chopper picked the group up at a prearranged spot and during the ride back to base, Green "fell" out.

The chopper pilot and his door gunners didn't see anything. They simply heard a yell and looked in time to see Lt. Green fall to his death.

Evidently Green always had the habit of standing near one of the open doors of the choppers in which they rode, and while that door gunner was distracted when one of the PRU supposedly pointed out something below, Green "fell".

The chopper pilot immediately turned and managed to land, and while the PRU established a perimeter, the body was recovered. Nothing else could ever be proven, a new DIOCC advisor was put in the District, and Lt. Green ceased to exist.

Clarkson said that of course it would not be reported as such in official documents. I'm sure Green was reported as killed in action and received a medal.

No, I did not like him, but he was an Army Lieutenant. I don't know if he had a family or not as I had never talked to him in any personal capacity. I do feel bad that he met his death in such a fashion, but "fragging" has always been one of the dangers a leader faces when leading men in battle.

In a business, you have to be prepared, be diligent, and constantly be on the lookout to take care of your employees' welfare or they, and you, could lose money. In a wartime situation, your "employees", face life and death situations daily, and thus their reactions to incompetence is proportionally greater.

Lt. Green paid the ultimate price for letting his employees down.

Chapter 13
R&R (REST AND RECUPERATION)

Every soldier in Viet Nam was entitled to one week of R&R after he had been in country for six months. The Army would fly him to Hawaii, Australia, Bangkok, Tokyo, or one of several other locations. The married men nearly always chose Hawaii and met their wives there. Most single men chose Bangkok or Australia because those places catered to the desires and pleasures of single men, and there were plenty of single women waiting for them.

The soldier was responsible for all expenses of the trip, except for his round trip air fare, which the Army provided, but most of the R&R sites gave substantial discounts to American service men. As I recall, everything in Hawaii was 50% off for those of us on R&R.

I know of a few men who worked at administrative positions in Saigon who took three and four R&R's, but this was typical of the Army. Those who did not need it, the rear echelon personnel, were the ones with the political and/or administrative clout to get more than one; while those who really needed more, were soldiers out in the jungle, and they carried no clout whatsoever and so only got one.

The Army did not pay for the plane fare of the spouses and since Hawaii was the closest to the states, and thus the cheapest air fare for the spouses, this was another reason married men went there.

I met Joeline there during December, 1968, after I had been in Viet Nam for seven months, and we naturally had a wonderful time. We spent three days in Honolulu and four days in Kauai.

I landed in Honolulu and was met by Joeline at the airport. We immediately got on another plane and flew to Kauai. I had once seen the movie South Pacific and thought that the scenery was beautiful, so I managed to reserve us a room at Hanalei Plantation, where the movie was actually filmed. That has to be one of the most beautiful spots in the world and the people on Kauai were extremely nice to us. We rented a jeep and visited many out of the way little stores and shops and were always treated with a smile and simple respect. We were often given a free pineapple when the owners learned I was on R&R. At one camera store the owner fixed a camera I had broken and refused to take any money for the repair. While the camera was being fixed, the owner's wife took Joeline out back and picked a beautiful orchid for her.

Kauai was absolutely one of the highlights of our life up to that point.

Our room, or bungalow, was huge and the walls facing the ocean were all glass from floor to ceiling and did not have curtains. If you wanted privacy, you pulled a curtain around the bed itself.

We were there in December and it rained every day, but that did not keep us from thoroughly enjoying ourselves. It did keep us off of the beach, but after spending seven months away from my wife, I was really not interested in going out there anyway.

After four days of solitude in Kauai, we flew back to Honolulu. The difference in the attitude of the people toward soldiers was amazing. As I said, I was treated with total respect and admiration on Kauai, but in Honolulu, the people looked at the soldiers on R&R as unwanted tourists and took our money without a smile, a thank you, or a pleasant Aloha. I found them to be rude and grouchy, but maybe I was left with that impression only because a cop there gave me a parking ticket.

Our hotel was, of course, right on the beach and the view was simply amazing. My only problem was trying to decide which to look at, and marvel at, the sunsets over the ocean or my wife standing on the deck in the outfits she had purchased for the occasion. She is 5'2" and at the time weighed 96 pounds. To give you an adequate picture, let me just say that very little of that weight was from her waist down. Today she is still beautiful, and still does not weight too much more than that.

Again, it rained continually for the entire time we were there, so we spent our time in the room, in restaurants, or shopping. We had many wonderful meals and the entertainment was first rate. We even managed to get a front row seat at a Don Ho performance and listened to him sing Tiny Bubbles only two years after it was released on record.

Today, when I look at the old pictures we took back then I still smile and remember fondly what a fantastic time we had, and how happy we were during those six days.

Of course, the knowledge that I was, in just a few days, going to have to return to Nam hung over us. But, we just shoved those thoughts aside and did not let them ruin a second of our time. We knew I had only five months left to serve and that fact made it bearable. I intentionally waited until I was a month past my half way point before taking the R&R. I wanted to make sure that when the R&R was over that we both understood I did not have as long left to serve as I had already served. Believe it or not, that really helped.

I could spend a month talking about how beautiful Joeline was and how great a time we had during that week, but those who went on an R&R already understand, and those who have not will never fully understand, so I'll just say that it was fantastic.

On our last night in Hawaii, we had a great, romantic dinner at a roof top restaurant. We lingered a long time after dinner, enjoying the moment and each other's company. Unfortunately, we lingered longer that we should have. When we left to get our car, the parking lot was locked and no one was around. Because of this, the next morning Joeline could not go to the base to see me off. She had to go to the parking garage of the restaurant and wait until it opened so she could get the car, turn it in to the rental agency, and then get to the airport to catch her own flight.

We stood there in the early dawn with a light mist falling, just holding onto each other and not saying a word. What was there to say? Good Bye? I love you? Be careful? We had said all of these things so many times there was just nothing appropriate left to say. Just holding tight to one another gave us both strength. Knowing how much she cared for me and that she would be waiting for me no matter what happened, gave me more courage and determination than all the military training the Army could provide.

Perhaps that is one reason the Army gave its soldiers these R&R's. They knew how much support from home could mean to their men. I know that I was certainly going back to that war with a renewed sense of purpose and will to survive. Joeline and I were going to have children and grandchildren and many years of being able to hold one another tightly. No Viet Cong was going to keep me from coming back to her.

That one single moment of standing in the middle of the street holding my wife lasted for what seemed a lifetime and yet, seemed to last only a split second. It is strange how time can be twisted and changed to fit one's perspective.

Finally the moment was over and we both knew it. We each got into a separate cab and they drove off in opposite directions, ending a week that will live in our memories forever.

I was so sad to be leaving her again it would be impossible to describe, but the only way to get something done, or to get the "clock" running was to get back and finish my job. So, in a way, I was happy, because I was starting the last part of my tour of duty.

While I am on the subject of R&R's I might as well tell you about Vick's.

Although I waited for seven months to take my R&R, my replacement, Vick, took his after only four months in country. Since he was single he elected to go to Australia, and even though his "vacation" has no real bearing on the war or on my story, it does point out the strange twists of fate that life throws in our way.

Upon his return to Tuy An after the R&R, he was a changed person. He was energetic, determined, had a goal in life, and wanted to work. He was in fact, in love. On his first night in Sydney, he met a girl in a bar. It's amazing what a girl can do to a guy!

The next six days were the happiest of his life. He spent every waking and sleeping hour with the girl, and her child. They toured the country together, stayed in the best hotels, and ate at all the best restaurants. She was pretty, lively, ambitious, and she instilled in Vick a reason for doing his job well, seeking advancement, and getting out of Viet Nam a better person.

He enlisted my aid in trying to figure out how he was going to manage to see her again. As I said, the Army only gave one R&R per person, and Vick was in no position to wrangle another one. When his year in Viet Nam was over, he would be shipped back to the states.

An air ticket to Australia is very expensive and Vick had no money. He vowed that he would save all of his next few pay checks, but l knew how difficult that would be. If he saved everything he earned, he would still not have enough to fly himself there and then all three of them back to the states.

During my last few months in country, Vick talked of very little else. However, during my last weeks I got the impression that his love for the girl was cooling - perhaps due to his failure to find any practical means of seeing her again. Besides, it was still going to be many months before he would be free of the Army, and since he had no college education, (he had received his commission through OCS and not through ROTC or a Military Academy) no real prospects after that.

In a letter I received after I had been back in the states for a few months, he told me of many things that had happened in Tuy An since my departure. He said that they had been digging a well in the compound and that in a week or so there would no longer be any need to haul water. In addition to that, they were building a patio and even a bathroom with flushing toilets; really modernizing the compound. But, as far as the war and his personal life were concerned, things were not going well. He did not, in the entire lengthy letter, mention the Australian girl.

In times of war many families are torn apart and destroyed. I was hoping that in this one case, the war might have brought three people together and formed a family. However, I am afraid that such things seldom happen in real life.

This is at a restaurant in Hawaii during R&R

Chapter 14
GARBAGE MAN

Perhaps, after reading this chapter, you will feel that it should have been left out of the book, especially if you have younger children reading. To be honest, I am not too certain that it should be here myself. However, if I am going to tell the truth about my experiences in Viet Nam, then I am compelled to tell the whole truth.

I have intentionally left out most of the hunger, starvation, sickness, disease, and depravity suffered by the general populace of the country. The American public does not want to read about such things, as it makes us squeamish and uneasy. Although starvation is a fact of life in hundreds of countries, we as Americans have generally been isolated from such conditions. The children in Viet Nam were not starving "to death" as children are in parts of African. There was simply too much rice grown in the country for that. However, hundreds of thousands of them literally had nothing. They could scrounge up enough to eat to keep them alive, but they had nothing more.

Since we, as Americans, had so much, these children felt it was OK to steal from us. If I left a jeep unguarded for only a few minutes it would be swept clean of anything loose, no matter how invaluable it seemed to me. I once had a toothbrush stolen from the compartment under the front seat of my jeep while I was buying supplies from a vendor in Tuy Hoa. An old man caught the culprit, a boy of about eight, and brought him up to me with the boy's arm twisted up behind his back. The man had me take hold of the boys arm and left. I have no idea what the heck I was supposed to do with him ~ shoot him for stealing a toothbrush that he was going to sell on the black market for food?

I released the boy and he was gone before I could even get my toothbrush back from him. Hunger is a very powerful, driving force and a little bit of food can be a tremendous bargaining tool. I can think of no better example of the truth of this statement than what happened in our garbage dump.

In our compound, the Americans divided up the weekly duties on a typically American schedule. We had a house boy who did little odd jobs, but the cooking, hauling water, and dumping the garbage were jobs we divided among ourselves. I suppose we could have taught our house boy to cook, but it was much easier to just do it ourselves. It took a jeep to haul the water and dump the garbage so we could not have the Vietnamese do those chores.

Cooking and hauling water were tasks I did not mind, but I hated hauling the garbage, and for a reason you would never imagine.

The dump was about three miles from our compound and was always swarming with Vietnamese children. When we pulled up in our jeep, pulling a trailer full of garbage cans, they would swarm from everywhere. Usually the cans were turned over and the contents scattered all over the jeep and trailer before we got to where we had intended to dump them. The kids would fight each other, push, shove, bite, and scratch, anything to get the choicest pieces of our garbage.

The heat caused items to spoil tremendously quickly and the smell was sometimes almost as unbearable as the sight of the starving kids. The situation could be handled in one of two ways, and I hated them both. First, we could simply let the kids go at it on the back of the trailer, spilling the rotting garbage everywhere and really making a mess of the trailer and jeep, which we would then have to drive to the river and then wash and clean them before returning to the compound. Or second, we could place an armed guard on the trailer and threaten to shoot the first kid who got too close to the trailer or jeep. The guard could not be bluffing. If need be, he would have to be willing to shoot, maybe not to kill, but shoot.

If the kids believed the guard would shoot, they would get as close as they dared and impatiently wait for one can to be dumped. Then they would dive for the contents. Unless we wanted to spend the day there we would have to dump the rest on top of them.

I stayed off of this detail as much as possible and was very relieved when Sgt. Burk, a member of the MACV team that was staying in the compound, started to volunteer to haul every load. It more or less became his permanent duty, and for a long time no one questioned it. As with any other unpleasant task someone voluntarily takes from you, you don't ask "why?" "Don't look a gift horse in the mouth", is the trite phrase most people would use.

Anyway, Burk had the job for over a month before the truth of the situation was revealed. I didn't like Burk. I could not prove it, but I was sure that he had been cheating in our poker games. I do know that he won a tremendous sum of money during the months he was in the compound. Of course I suppose that could have been the reason I didn't like him. He beat me at poker.

I was looking for Corporal James one afternoon and was told he had been going with Burk to dump garbage. That evening I took James as my radio man on a very simple, and safe, operation. I didn't expect any VC where we were going, but was going out to break in two new members of the PRU.

After the ambushes were set, I took James into the middle of the perimeter and confronted him. I told him I wanted to know what was going on with Burk and the garbage. At first he tried to lie to me, but it did no good. He was an inexperienced Corporal and I could read him like a book. I told him to cut out the crap and tell me what I wanted to know.

After only a few moments, he told me the story. According to him, Burk would drive up to the dump with his M16 across his legs and evidently, after his first trip, the kids knew better than to come near him. The rumor was that he had shot two of them the first time he ran the route. Anyway, he allowed a young girl to come up to the jeep - James called her Garbage Annie - she would give Sgt. Burk a blow job and then he would let her sift thru the garbage cans before he dumped them.

Burk had James go along to hold an M16 on the other kids till the girl was finished. Hardly a pretty picture of an American soldier, but it shows how low some people can sink.

The whole affair involving Sgt. Burk didn't surprise me, but the Corporal's being involved did, and I told him so. He knew the power I could muster in the district and was really afraid. I used the same line that Carlson had used with me once, that a court martial would be the least of his troubles when I got through with him. I asked him what Burk had on him. I knew there must be something because there couldn't be two such scumbags in the same district.

The poor kid really broke down. He told me that on his first patrol after getting here he had been with Sgt. Burk. They were on a search and destroy mission with one of Be's Army units. The Major was along as an advisor and James was carrying his radio. Burk and James somehow got separated from the Major as they entered a hamlet, just as a fire fight broke out. James was petrified and began shooting. He said he accidentally hit a woman of the village who ran out in front of him. A couple of VC were killed as the sweep continued through the adjoining rice patties. Burk told James that if it ever came out that he had killed this "innocent" villager, then he would be tried for murder.

When James objected to going along on Burks's garbage runs, Burk used the incident to force him to go.

I was almost sorry I had asked. Now, I had to determine if James was guilty of anything. I had to find out if it was a justified shooting, an accident, or whether it was in fact a criminal act on his part. If it was, the poor kid was in real trouble, because I would not let it go. Next, I would have to deal with Burk.

It would have been a lot easier if I had just kept my mouth shut and minded my own business.

After a few days of having Gem talk to Be and other members of Be's Army unit, I found that the mission in question had been in a free fire area north of Highway 1. This in itself just about relieved James of any guilt, because Be had declared that anyone living or working there was a VC and should be shot on sight. The villagers had been warned to stay out of the area and of the consequences should they choose to disobey.

Before I could personally talk to any of Be's troops, I had to get his permission. I explained what I was looking into and that I was not questioning any of his troops' actions, but I had to find out how one of the Americans had responded to the operation in question. He had no objection as long as he could be present when I interviewed them. He sent a messenger to get the guy who had commanded that particular movement.

While that was being done, I had Gem go through our files and get me all the information we had on that particular operation. The first thing he found was that Hung had been there. I found that Hung happened to be in the compound right then, so I sent for him.

When I asked why he had gone on what was obviously not a normal PRU operation, he said he had gone along as a sort of bodyguard for the major.

I asked him if he could remember what had happened on the mission.

He said there was a minor skirmish and that as far as he could remember four VC had been killed and one of the RF soldiers (Regular Force - Be's Army unit) had been wounded, and might have died later. He couldn't remember for sure whether the guy had died or not.

That didn't concern me, so I asked if he knew whether one of the VC had been a woman. He thought for a while and said that he was sure they were all men.

He left, and a few moments later the Vietnamese operations officer came in with his records. Gem read them and said that there had been five VC killed during the raid, all males. He said one female had been treated for a bullet wound in her shoulder. She was questioned at the scene a little later, but released. According to him, she was "nothing," she didn't matter to anyone, so he let her go. She had promised to stay out of that area and to stop working for the enemy.

I asked the guy if he remembered the American radio operator being along. He said he did, but that he, James, left with the major right after the fire fight as they were trailing the VC who had escaped the village. The commander had left a squad in the village to search it and that is when they found the wounded woman.

I called James in and told him the good news. At first he was tremendously relieved, then he got mad. Burk had told him the woman was dead and he had believed it all of this time. He wanted to confront Burk, but I convinced him that if he did the entire matter would come out and the shooting incident would go on his record. I convinced him that I would take care of Burk, and that his name would not be involved.

Having taken care of James, I turned my attention to Burk. I went to the Major and told him of Burk's garbage runs, leaving out the fact that James had been accompanying him. He asked if there were any witnesses and since I did not want to involve James, I told him no.

Then he wanted to know how I knew about it if there were no witnesses.

I told him some of the villagers had complained to Gem.

He said that since there were no reliable witnesses and since Be was not reporting or complaining about the incident, there was nothing he could do, but that he would see that Burk did not go on any more garbage runs. "Besides," he said, "she's only Vietnamese trash." (He was really proud of his little play on words.) "And, Burk wasn't forcing her to do anything she didn't want to do."

I got so mad I could hardly contain myself. "Mad as a wet hen" was an old expression my mom would have used. I couldn't say much else to the major without getting myself in trouble, so I decided to do something I had never done before, I went over his head. I took the mail chopper to Tuy Hoa and went to Mr. Clarkson. I explained the whole thing and told him that he had better get Burk out of our District or I would take care of Burk myself. I didn't really know what I meant by that, but it seemed the thing to say.

Remember that Clarkson was a civilian and really had no say in regard to Army matters. But, he was a civilian who just happened to work for the CIA - at least I always assumed that is who he worked for. He certainly never told me he did, but the money I got to pay the informants came from the CIA, supposedly, and Clarkson gave me that money. So?

Anyway Clarkson made a call, talked to someone for a few minutes, hung up, and said Burk would be out of the compound by the time I got back there the next afternoon. Burk had only four months left in country, but he would spend those four months as a platoon sergeant with an infantry unit.

With Burk gone, we once again divided the garbage detail and Garbage Annie moved on to a more lucrative profession. According to Gem, she became a hooker in Tuy Hoa. The major had an idea that I might have had something to do with Burk's transfer, but he never asked me directly and I certainly didn't volunteer the information.

It has always been my philosophy that we reap what we sow. I have seen it happen time and time again, where someone does something that is morally wrong or that hurts someone else and even if they aren't punished immediately and seem to get away with it, they eventually get what's coming to them. I know that I am naïve, but I really believe that "Right" wins out in the long run. As for Sgt. Burk, he definitely paid for his sins.

One day, just before I left Viet Nam for the last time, Clarkson sent me a note concerning Sgt. Burk. It seems that one night, after being with an infantry unit for a month he had been caught cheating at poker. The next day he had been shot during a fire fight. It could not be proven, but everything seemed to indicate that he had been shot by one of his own men.

Lt. Green and now Sgt. Burk? I know I said that things seem to work out on their own, but I have also noticed that sometimes they get a little help in getting worked out. Both of these guys were in Clarkson's area, and under his "radar". I had always been very careful in regard to my actions around him and in my reports to him, but I began to wonder if maybe I had better spend even more time "walking on egg shells" anytime I was dealing with him. This guy may have been way more than he seemed.

I suddenly remembered what he had said to me one time about a court martial being the least of my worries and I realized that maybe I had more to fear in Viet Nam than the Viet Cong. Mr. Clarkson might be the most dangerous individual in that entire country.

Chapter 15
A NIGHT AMBUSH

Some operations, such as the cave incident with the Chu Hoa, went off without a hitch and we had tremendous successes, while others were nothing short of living nightmares.

All of my pre-Viet Nam training had to do with Search and Destroy missions. These were Platoon, Company and even Battalion size operations. Our training had to do with perimeter defense, patrolling, and methods and procedures for destroying large enemy operations. All of which would have been great had I been sent to the 4th Infantry Division, but in my particular situation they were of little use.

I had to come up with my own set of rules for troop deployment, usage and safety. Gem was a great asset and I used him to sift through my plans of action and tell me which he felt were good and which were impractical, or impossible. He had a good head for jungle tactics and most importantly he was sensible enough to want to get out of the war alive.

Hung, on the other hand, would agree to any plan that carried with it the possibility of killing VC, while Gem would vote no on any that he felt carried with it any unnecessary risks.

With Gem's overly cautious tactical advice, Hung's aggressive attitude toward the VC and his knowledge of jungle tactics, combined with my knowledge of people and common sense, we usually made a terrific team. But, on one occasion I actually planned an operation without any of their input, in fact, I planned it without their knowledge and it ended up being tremendously successful.

A Korean Corporal had come to our compound to seek my help on an operation his superiors had in mind. I have told you of the one operation I planned and carried out with combined Korean and Vietnamese troops and it was a miserable failure. So, needless to say, I was very skeptical of trying another one.

Later, I found out that some Korean big wigs were upset because the Americans and Vietnamese in the district were achieving great success while the Korean contingent in the District had received no positive publicity and had very little success in neutralizing any VC. I could have told them why:

> The Koreans had the most secure compound in all of Phu Yen Province and all they did was sit behind their fortifications, concertina wire, and mines. On the one operation I got them involved in they did everything in their power to make sure no VC came near us.

> As I said before, this is certainly no knock on Korean soldiers in general. Soldiers are only as good, and only as affective as their leaders allow them to be. The Korean leaders in this unit were either lazy, or afraid. I would have loved to have some of their soldiers under my command as they are usually great fighters.

Obviously, this new offer to work together was made only because the camp commander had been ordered to do so. He complied with his orders by sending someone to ask me for help. But, his only sending a Corporal was unheard of, even to the point of being ridiculous. He probably felt that I would be insulted by this and fail to respond. Thus he could tell his superiors that he had requested that I work with him, but that I had refused.

This guy obviously did not know how badly I wanted VC.

I asked the Corporal point blank why he had been sent and one of his officers had not come. He sheepishly explained that all of his superiors wanted my help very much, but were too tied up at the moment to come and ask for it.

Crud, I really didn't care. The District was in such turmoil that I would take what I could get. We were both after the same thing, and if my going to their compound and pretending I needed help would get me a little cooperation then I would go.

When we finally passed through all their barricades and arrived at their Headquarters, we were met by a Major who smiled, welcomed me, and asked me to accompany him. The Corporal who had come to get me disappeared and I never saw him again.

We walked into a control room and everyone in it sprang to attention. I was offered a seat, tea, and asked to wait a few minutes. The Major left and then returned a few moments later with a Colonel.

Again the room sprang to attention. The military discipline in the Korean Compound was something to see. And, by the way, the Corporal was never mentioned - there was no apology, no attempt to explain why he had been sent; it was as if I had come alone, on a mission of my own.

The Colonel introduced himself, with the aid of an interpreter, and asked how he could help me. I tried to say that I had been sent for, and that l assumed they wanted my help.

The Colonel's reply would have done credit to our country's politicians. He said that yes, he did know about my operations – my attempts to catch VCI - and yes he would be happy to cooperate on a combined American, Vietnamese, and Korean operation. He said he would take me to his intelligence section and assured me that I would have their full cooperation and all the "help" I needed.

I understood. The Koreans were going to help me clear up "my problem". Oh well, as long as I got the information I wanted and the help I needed, who cared about semantics.

I was taken into another room where we were again served tea. At least I thought it was going to be tea. It was heated and it was served in tea cups, but after one sip I realized it was definitely not tea. I don't know what it was called, but we spent the next hour sipping some kind of a heated Korean liquor.

Their intelligence officer came in and with the aid of the interpreter and the liquor we formulated some sort of maneuver involving the Koreans, the Vietnamese, and my PRU. But, by the time we were finished I really wasn't too clear on the specifics.

I was raised at "brush tracks", (small race tracks) throughout Arkansas and Oklahoma, where jugs of White Lightning were always being passed around. Whatever this Korean drink was, any Ozark Moonshiner would have been proud to claim it for his own. Man, that stuff was strong.

I drove back to our compound, took a shower to clear my head, and then went to see Be. Although I tried to sound positive and upbeat, my one previous adventure with one of these combined operations left me less than thrilled to do another one. To make sure that I was not wasting my time again, I had come up with my own plan that I did not tell anyone about. No one but Be, of course. I knew better than to try something in his District without his knowledge, and besides if anything went wrong, I was definitely going to need his help.

It was difficult to explain to him what I wanted to do without an interpreter, but I really wanted to keep this secret, so I managed without Gem. What I was planning to do was going to be very dangerous for me and my men, and if it was not successful, and if we got into trouble, it was not going to be because someone leaked information.

The Vietnamese were to start a sweep from the Eastern edge of a particularly dangerous section of the jungle to the north of Tuy An.

The Koreans were to sweep, starting from the Western edge of the area. We would perform a pincer movement, with the idea being that any VC would be crushed between the two forces.

I had thoroughly checked my files and did not feel we would have much luck getting any VCI. I couldn't find any informant reports of any of the ones I wanted working that far away from the populace, but these trails were so deep in VC territory, and so many of those trails led into VC valley, that I felt that with the secret part of my plan, and by using the PRU only, we had a better than average chance of getting some action.

If my superiors in Saigon asked, I would simply stretch the truth and tell them that I had a report of a large contingent of VCI working out of that area.

I was counting on the Korean and Vietnamese RF soldiers on the mission to behave the way they had before when I put them together. The Korean commander had basically used me the last time, so I was using him and his troops this time. Seemed fair to me. The hardest part of setting this up was getting Be to let me use his troops as decoys, but he wanted VC and he finally agreed that I might get some if my plan worked.

At 0600 hour on the morning of the operation we were still standing around the compound. We had been ready to go since 0500, but for some reason we had not moved. I finally managed to find Be and asked him what the delay was. He said he would not leave until after the Koreans had left their compound. He would not place his troops in front of theirs. He didn't trust them.

I frantically drove to the Korean compound and tried to find out what was causing their delay. I was told that they were waiting on the Vietnamese, as was the plan, and they would not change it and go first.

I drove back to Be and explained to him that since this was his District, the Koreans were giving his troops the honor of leading the mission and going first. I explained that it was an honor to lead, that it meant the Koreans had to follow him. He liked that explanation and gave the order for his men to move out. .

Once out of the compounds, the two contingents went to their pre-assigned jump off points and began their treks through the jungles.

The MACV commander in the compound at the time and I flew air cover in choppers for a while and witnessed a wild scene. The entire operation worked like it was led by a drunken Corporal. The Vietnamese contingent strolled along the trails and dikes of the rice paddies, just as if they were on a walk in a park. They obviously felt that there were enough of them that they were in no danger, they sent scouts out to search for mines, and the rest of them just enjoyed the walk. Very reminiscent of the last time I traveled with an RF company.

The Koreans on the other hand, marched in a column of 3's at a double time pace. They were obviously more concerned with getting to the meeting point first, than they were of tangling with any VC. I suppose that to them, getting there first would mean that they had won - they would have beaten the Vietnamese in their own jungle.

Both groups stayed out of the dense jungle, where the VC would be and traveled on small roads and trails that my troops and I would never be dumb enough to travel along. Doing so was asking to be blown up or ambushed.

I had the pilot set me down in a clearing next to the Vietnamese contingent and joined Hung and the rest of the PRU, who, much to their chagrin; I had asked to accompany these units. Hung was thoroughly disgusted, and really gave me a dirty look, but when I assured him we would get the action he wanted, when we split off. He looked at me and grinned.

A few days before when I had first asked him and the PRU to go along on the mission, he had looked at me inquiringly. I hadn't said anything else, but I'm sure he knew me well enough to know I had something in mind, but now, after an hour or so with these units he had probably started to wonder if maybe I had lost my mind. Now, however, he caught on very quickly and was reassured.

An hour later we reached the meeting point. The Koreans were lined up, as if for a parade. The Vietnamese straggled in by one's and two's at their own pace. The two company commanders met, saluted and started back south on separate paths.

Hung, Gem, the rest of the PRU and I melted into the jungle. We silently traveled a mile or so and then set up a perimeter so Hung and I could talk and I could explain my plan. I told him that in my opinion, because of reports his informants had been giving me, there was a VC force somewhere in this area. Of course they would have gotten wind of the two large forces going through, but I was counting on them thinking that everyone had left the area. I hoped they would relax and maybe let down their guard a little. I told Hung we should give them a surprise. He loved the idea.

134

We stayed in hiding for an hour and then silently advanced into the thick triple canopy jungle to a spot we had chosen on the map to set up our ambush. After studying the area, it did not look as good as it did on the map, so I decided to go a little further. By chance we came upon a perfect ambush site.

It was a trail crossing that showed signs of considerable usage. By now we were on the edge of an area we called VC Valley because we knew that there were trails here that NVA soldiers used when traveling from Hanoi to Saigon. It was an area on which the air force dropped large bombs whenever they received reports that large units were traveling through. We never did get reports of them hitting much, and it did not deter the enemy from using the area, but I guess it made Saigon feel better. This was the same general area where the Chu Hoa had led us months before.

We were miles from any villages and if we jumped anything it would not be the average wandering VC bands. One of the trails came from the north and continued on south, while another headed toward Highway #1 and the coast.

I sent four PRU down the south trail and Hung set the remaining men up in an ambush position along the trail coming from the north and along the small clearing in front of us.

I set up four claymores covering the trail and the clearing, spaced everyone out, checked our fields of fire, and settled down to wait darkness and the long night that lay ahead of us.

This was not an area to play around in. Hung and I went over the maps very carefully and made sure everyone knew our exit routes, our regrouping points and all of our passwords and silent signals. Hung went from man to man and checked each one separately. We left as little to chance as we could.

While I had been on the chopper with the Colonel, I told him I had planned to stay behind with my PRU and we were going to run a little operation of our own. He had no idea how to react. He had not been in country long enough to understand what my duties really were, but he had been told that I knew what I was doing and to let me alone to do my job - which was killing VCI.

He knew enough to ask if this was a VCI operation. I lied and said of course.

Now that we were set, I called him on the radio and used the simple code I had devised for this one mission to give our coordinates and confirm that he had prearranged air support should we need it. As I said, I was leaving nothing in my power to chance. If we got hit with more than we could handle, I wanted the air force to be ready to back us up.

After that, there was nothing to do but get as comfortable as possible and wait. The heat was oppressive and the bugs and mosquitoes thick. Hung, who was about 10 yards from me, held up a large snake he had evidently just killed and this did nothing to comfort me. I kept asking myself what the heck I was doing out this far in VC territory with less than 20 men for protection, and could not give myself an adequate answer. Of course, these men were very experienced, knew what they were doing, and would never run from a fight. But, I kept thinking, "I wish I had a company of Army Rangers or Marines with me". Or, I could simply be back in the compound under my mosquito net reading the latest letter from my wife.

Darkness finally fell.

Hung had prearranged when each man could sleep and when each was to be awake. I was free to doze whenever I wanted. It will be hard for most people to believe it, but I managed to doze on and off until a little after 2300 hours, when Hung appeared near me and held up two fingers. Two people had entered the ambush.

I simply nodded to Hung, indicating the ambush should go per standard operating procedure. In other words, the two men would be quietly dispatched by the four PRU members whom we had left 25 yards on down the trail. They knew that if we let a small number of VC pass, then we expected them to quietly kill them and pull them off the trail. If we let more than four pass, then the PRU were to also let them pass.

A moment later two men in black pajamas came into my field of vision. They were walking quietly and stealthily. They walked within ten feet of me. One looked directly at my hiding position, then moved on.

136

Now I was definitely not sleepy. These did not look like your average, every day, VC. These looked more like experienced NVA scouts. We could be in very serious trouble.

Five long, disquieting moments later, which seemed to be hours, Hung held up nine fingers. This was the moment of decision. This could be, and probably was, the main element, and we should blow the claymores and spring the ambush. Yet, 1 hesitated. We were far into VC territory and those soldiers who passed earlier were probably part of a much larger group. We had to be very, very careful here. Why would they be this far away from the civilian populace unless they were just traveling through? And if they were doing so, they could be part of the NVA Regiment that Saigon had been getting reports was moving south from Hanoi.

Hung impatiently held up the nine fingers again as the first of the men came into my view. It was very dark under the jungle canopy, but there was enough moonlight for me to see the men when they walked to within about 20 yards of me. I held out my hand with my thumb up. I was letting them pass. I had to hope that the PRU down the trail could neutralize them when we did spring the main ambush. Otherwise, we would have nine well trained enemy soldiers behind us.

The area I had chosen for the ambush was perfect. We were well concealed in the thick jungle, but in our field of fire was a clearing through which the jungle trail ran. Ordinarily no one would walk through such an area, but 1 had relied on the fact that the enemy in this area would feel secure at night. They knew there were no large scale US Army units in the area, and no one else would be crazy enough to bother them out here. The darkness and canopy jungle kept them from worrying about gunships.

A few moments after the nine soldiers had walked past, Hung lay silently by my side. I knew that he was thinking that I had let a golden opportunity pass to get a bunch of NVA regulars. But, then suddenly he started grinning as he looked at me and motioned with his head. I looked and saw what he was grinning about, but I certainly did not grin. There were many, many soldiers, in NVA uniforms coming through the clearing and down the trail. There were a lot of them.

I got ready to blow the claymores, but then hesitated, we were about to engage a unit of the NVA. I was not excited, as Hung was. I was scared to death. But, I had no choice. There were so many of them and they were spread out so far that they could be literally walking over us in a few seconds.

As they advanced through the clearing, I set off the claymores. We sprayed the area for approximately ten seconds and many of the PRU threw hand grenades. Then we all withdrew into the jungle and quickly headed for our prearranged area before we could be overrun by the huge force that was probably behind the soldiers we hit.

By the time we all arrived we could hear the sound of many men moving, firing, and shouting back at the ambush site. From all the noise it was easy to tell that there had been many more behind those we had ambushed.

We quickly took off for our second assembly area about a mile away. When we reached the deserted hamlet we had decided upon earlier in the evening we counted heads, and found that we had again not lost a man. The four men we had sent down the trail had actually beaten us to the hamlet.

We set off again. This time as one group, and wasted no time in clearing the area. As we walked I called the Colonel and explained the situation. I told him that in my opinion there was a large NVA unit heading south from the coordinates I gave him and suggested he call an immediate bomb drop. Or he could call in artillery, we just weren't about to leave anyone near there to direct the fire.

By the time we reached our final rendezvous point and had set up a protective perimeter in a relatively secure area where we would spend the rest of the night, the air force had arrived and was shelling the area around our ambush site, by now a couple of miles from where we were.

I have been told that when the Army brought in an Infantry unit a few days later, they searched the area and from the bodies and information they gathered, it was determined that we had definitely attacked the NVA Regiment that was known to be heading to the Saigon area. They were coming directly from Hanoi.

It did not get me any VCI, and it did not get me any of the VC that had been causing us serious problems in our own district. But, we had just successfully attacked an entire NVA Regiment with 20 men and had not suffered a single casualty in doing so. There were thousands more of them coming down from Hanoi, so we did not really accomplish anything militarily, but we sure felt like we had had a good night.

Chapter 16
SWIFT BOATS

"Did you nearly get killed", or "When was the closest you came to getting killed?" is a question that every war veteran is often asked.

For me, that question could have but one answer: The time I went on a patrol that originated with the United States Navy.

Shortly after his arrival in Tuy An, Major Lee, the new top American MACV advisor in the district, called me into his office and asked me to go along on, and help him set up, an operation with the Navy. He told me that he had received word from Provincial headquarters in Tuy Hoa that he was to accompany a Vietnamese unit on a joint American Navy, Vietnamese operation, using RF troops. He said he knew that it was not in my normal range of duties, but he laughed and said that working with the Navy was certainly not normal for him either. He said that I knew the troops and the area and was basically asking me nicely for my help.

I could not imagine why anyone in Tuy Hoa was trying to organize an operation in our District and I asked him about it. He just said that there were some Navy Swift Boat recently assigned to our area and each of the districts along the coast were being asked to cooperate with, and use them.

I was even more surprised when Dai Uy Be gave his approval for the Major to use some of his troops. This was the first and only operation that I ever heard of which originated outside of our district, but took place inside of it. Be normally insisted on running his own district and allowed no interference

I questioned him about his going along with this request, but he just smiled and said it would be an interesting experience for his troops. I asked him what he thought of the U.S. Navy being involved in his district and he said, "Your Navy should stay out in the ocean where it belongs".

Arranging a relatively large scale operation against the VC from the ocean was totally new to me. I searched reports and found a few that indicated a VC presence in a relatively inaccessible area along the coast. It was a place that could only be reached by helicopters and I had not deemed it worth my time to try to arrange such an operation. However, swift boats should be able to get to the same area and it might be a surprise for the VC in that area. So, I got it all arranged.

Two Navy swift boats picked us up very early a few mornings later. We piled on and sat anywhere we could find a spot and something to hold on to. They were neat little boats, extremely quick and armed with two 50 caliber machine guns and an 81mm mortar. The Navy men were a happy bunch. They just patrolled up and down the coast firing at anything in free fire areas and docking at a safe port every night - quite a safe and leisurely way to spend a war. I envied them. These boats were extremely fast and a blast to ride. The only thing lacking was water skis or boggie boards.

When we reached our destination they got us as near to the beach as possible, then informed us we would have to jump off and wade the rest of the way in due to the reefs. The first Vietnamese soldier to jump off carried a 30 caliber machine gun. He went under the rough water and didn't come up.

I handed my M16 to Gem and jumped in. The water came up to my chin when I stood on my tip toes and 1 was having trouble keeping my balance in the surf. I stuck my head under water and saw the poor Vietnamese soldier standing next to me, but even the top of his head was underwater. He was still clutching the 30 caliber, the weight of which obviously kept him down. But, he would not let go of the machine gun and swim for the surface. Gem told me later that any Vietnamese soldier who lost a machine gun would be shot by Dai Uy Be. I guess this guy was just going to drown rather than face the wrath of Be.

I stuck my head under water again, pried his fingers off the gun, and walked gingerly to the shore with it. He showed up a few minutes later, weakly smiled his thanks, took back his load and sat down on a rock to clean the salt out of it and dry it off.

Not a very auspicious beginning to an operation, and I had a feeling it was just a portent of things to come. As things turned out, I should have trusted my instincts and climbed right back on the swift boat. The entire operation was a total failure and almost got me and my radio man killed.

By the time we got everyone ashore, saved many of the Vietnamese from drowning in the surf, dried and cleaned out the weapons, and started on a sweep, any VC for miles around would have been long gone. The only thing that probably kept us from getting clobbered on the beach was the swift boats and their 50 caliber machine guns sitting just off the shore. I had been told that these guys were very accurate with their weapons and no one in their right mind wants to be shot with a 50 cal.

After sweeping the area for a few hours and finding nothing, we decided to call it day and head back. When we reached the beach, we found that the boats were even further out to sea. They radioed in that they could not get any closer due to the tide.

We had three choices. We could drown half of the Vietnamese trying to get out to the boats, walk most of the night to get back to our own compound, or set up a perimeter, with the swift boats as added protection, and spend the night where we were, and get back on the boats close to shore the next morning.

Personally l wanted to stay where we were, but the Major overruled me. He did not relish the idea of spending the night out of our compound with only a small number of RF soldiers for protection.

I knew that setting up a perimeter with these troops and spending the night was much safer than trying to walk back in the dark, but he insisted that activity was better than a passive lack of activity, so we were going to walk. As I said before, I always felt this area was only accessible by helicopter, so obviously if it was hard to get to, it was going to be just as difficult to get out of, especially at night.

Our next decision was based on expediency. We could go overland, which would take most of the night, or we could trot along the beach. This was obviously a much faster way to travel, but very susceptible to an enemy ambush.

After conferring with the swift boats, the major decided to take to the beach and have the boats fire into the jungle at the edge of the beach, 50 yards ahead of our point men. That way the VC could not set up an ambush ahead of us. We hoped. The only problem with this arrangement was that our Vietnamese point men refused to walk along the beach with the boats firing just ahead of them.

Gem told me that a few years before, a swift boat had killed a couple of soldiers in the district and that no one trusted them. Finally, two of the soldiers agreed to walk point if I went with them. I suppose they felt the Navy would be more careful if there was an American present. I took Clack, with his radio, and we started off.

Everything went fine for perhaps an hour then all hell broke loose. My whole world seemed to erupt in flying sand and bullets. We tried to bury ourselves in the sand as the beach flew up around us. My first instinct, after I had flattened myself on the ground, was to fire into the trees along the edge of the beach, where I supposed the attack was coming from. This I did without any conscious mental effort, but as my finger squeezed off an automatic burst, my mind kept working on other things. It's hard to say which thoughts came first as they all just flashed through my brain at seemingly the same instant.

I knew to lie on the sand, in the open, and fire at a hidden enemy was suicide. I knew we had to jump up and attack the ambush. I knew it was probably suicidal to stand up. And then, almost at the same instant, I knew that the shots were not coming from the jungle.

I flung myself over to where Clack was lying with his face buried in the sand and grabbed the hand set off his radio. We were on the swift boat frequency so I pulled the trigger on the mike and began yelling,

"Cease Fire! Cease Fire!" with all the energy, excitement, and fear of a man who knows he is about to be torn apart by 50 caliber shells.

The sand instantly stopped exploding, the Vietnamese stopped firing and all was quiet. You've heard of the quiet before a storm, well this was the quiet after one. I doubt that anyone was breathing, I know that I wasn't. Then I exploded into the mike, "What the hell are you guys trying to do, kill us all?"

A quiet, calm voice came back with one word, "Sorry".

Miraculously no one had been killed, probably because there were only four of us at point, and we were several yards apart. Most of the shells (they were really bullets, but if you have ever seen a 50 caliber bullet, it looks like an artillery shell) simply tore up the sand around us. One of the Vietnamese had been hit, and half of his thigh had been torn off, and Clack had been temporarily blinded by sand which had been thrown into his eyes by a near miss.

The boat Captain later explained what had happened. One of his gunners had been firing ahead of us with one of the 50 calibers. It was very dark, so the boat captain had been using the starlight scope on board to direct the gunner, who could not see us. The first gun had begun to get hot, so the Captain walked over to the other side of the boat and pointed to where we were for the second gunner. This man thought that where the Captain pointed was where he wanted him to aim. So he started firing there.

The Captain had put down his scope and didn't see what was going on as we received the fire. Evidently the gunner had only fired for a few seconds or so before the Captain realized what was happening. He was stopping the gunner at about the same time I began yelling on the radio.

We doctored the wounded man, put him on a litter and were ready to start again. At least I was. The Vietnamese, however, refused to move along the sand again with the swift boats for cover.

The Major and I checked our maps and decided we had come far enough that now we could turn inland and still could possibly reach Phu Tan by 2 in the morning - sorry, 0200. There we would spend the rest of the night and enter the compound in at first light.

The swift boat captain again apologized and said they would be standing by off shore if there was anything they could do to help us.

145

After crossing one hill and coming close to the top of another, the point men signaled for us to stop and get down. Then they signaled for me to come forward. I took Clack with me.

The moon had come up, the clouds had scattered, and the valley below was bathed in moonlight . As I peered over the crest, the reason for our stopping became obvious. At least thirty VC were gathered in a field below us. I cannot imagine what they were doing standing out in the open like that, but I was sure not going to miss the chance to correct their error in judgment

I called the swift boat Captain and asked how accurate his mortar crew was. He wanted to make amends and said they were the best in the Navy. This didn't comfort me much. How many Navy men know anything about mortars?

After fixing the coordinates on my map, I told him to fire one and then I would give him one quick correction and then he should fire for effect.

The first shell landed about 100 yards past the majority of the VC and l quickly gave him an adjustment.

The Captain was right, his men were good. The VC were obviously scattering after the first shell hit, but the next three rounds fell among them. I gave him another correction and then I was poked in the ribs by Clack. The Major was motioning that he wanted us back with him. I supposed he wanted to know what was going on.

Clack sent the point men on ahead and indicated that they were to stay on this side of the hill. We didn't want to tangle with what was left of the VC. We had had enough for one night.

He and I then started to jog back down the hill to where the Major and the rest of the troops were waiting for us. We had gone about 20 yards when the ground seemed to come up to meet us. I was thrown flat and had the wind was knocked out of me. Clack had been a little ahead of me and wasn't hurt. He quickly came back and helped me, gasping for air, to my feet.

It took a few minutes for me to get my breath back and realize what had happened. I looked back to where we had been, and the small tree, behind which we had been kneeling to direct the fire, was gone.

In its place was a small, smoking hole. About then, my buddy the swift boat Captain, came back on the air and asked where that last shell had landed. It seems that, although the boat had some sort of stabilizer on board, they had hit a large swell just as the mortar was fired, and the shell had been thrown off course.

Had Clack and I not started back to the Major when we had, what was left of my body would have been plastered around that hole, and I would not be writing this today.

I was so stunned I was not even mad. I simply told the guy to cease fire, thanked him for his work, and wished him and his men good luck during the rest of their tour of duty.

After going through hundreds of fire fights and ambushes without getting a scratch, I was nearly blown away twice in one night by my own Navy, and the night was not even over.

For the next hour, I walked in the middle of the group. Then we stopped, and before the major even sent for me to come to the front of the column, I knew what the problem was.

The reason I had neglected this area, and had considered it impassible was because of a huge wall of impenetrable bamboo. I had seen it once from the other side of the wall and at that time, months ago, could not find a way through it. On one side, were vertical cliffs of rock along the coast. Then the bamboo wall stretched for miles away from the ocean. To go around it would take us hours and hours. I knew we were eventually going to hit this wall and was ready to tell the Major that this was why I did not want to try to walk back to Phu Tan.

But as soon as I got to the wall one of the RF soldiers came up to Gem and began explaining something to him. Gem translated that this soldier was from this area and knew a way through the bamboo. I basically told him, "lead on McDuff".

Amazingly he actually did. He walked right up to what I thought was a solid wall of bamboo, bent down a little, continued walking and disappeared. We all followed, one at a time. The major, Clack, and I really had to bend over. In fact, we were basically on our hands and knees for most of the way through.

The guy evidently knew exactly where he was going. We crawled through this stuff and it was like going through a very elaborate and very constricting maze. We had huge bamboo all around us. This stuff was 6" to 8" in diameter and as solid as if they were steel rods. However, once you were inside the wall, there was what seemed to be a small animal trail that weaved right and left, back and forth, and I suppose if you did not know which turn to take you could spend the rest of your life in there. It was horribly hot and humid. This was late at night, and I really feel that if anyone ever got stuck in there during the day, they would quickly die of heat stroke. There was absolutely no wind, and hardly any air inside the grove. This was about a 30 foot wall that I thought was totally impenetrable.

Amazingly, we reached the other side within 15 minutes and were able to continue our marvelous adventure. We finally reached Phu Tan and set up a protective perimeter. I offered to keep watch until dawn and let the Major get a little sleep, but he said I must be crazy if I thought he could sleep out there.

I said that that was fine with me, crawled onto a straw mat offered to me by one of the Vietnamese and quickly went to sleep. Unfortunately, I forgot that once things start to go badly, they usually continue to do so. I woke up at dawn to find that I had been nearly eaten alive by either bed bugs, fleas or mosquitoes. They had left me with bites all over my body.

What a night!

Chapter 17
A SHORT LIFE

Have you ever noticed that sometimes, very unusual things trigger your mind into dredging up strange memories from your past that have nothing to do with what you are doing in the present? I am told that everything you have ever seen, heard, or smelled is still locked away someplace in your brain, but finding the right key to the retrieval process is difficult. I can be introduced to someone and three minutes later I will have no clue what his/her name is. But, suddenly the name of some kid I knew in the third grade will come to me, seemingly for no reason at all.

Today, 44 years after leaving Viet Nam, the sound of a helicopter passing overhead always triggers something in my mind and I get a shiver of apprehension every time I hear that sound. Yet, I can watch a war movie and not be bothered at all. The mind picks strange things to trigger it, but sounds and smells seem to be excellent catalysts.

I was walking through a market in Guatemala the other day and some smell that I could not even identify came drifting to me. It tripped something so vivid and strong in my subconscious that I had to check my surroundings to determine where l was and make sure that my past had not overtaken my present.

Years ago, I was watching an old rerun of a MASH TV episode with my son, Tomey. The episode being shown was one where "Hot Lips" was talking to an injured young soldier who was lying on a stretcher. The doctors had already told her that the boy was going to die within a few hours. The soldier did not know he was about to die and was telling her what he was going to do when he got home. My son said, "That must be terrible situation for her to be in. Shouldn't she tell him he doesn't have but a very short time to live? Maybe he would want to know so that he could be praying or something".

That question immediately brought back a memory that I had suppressed for many years, a memory that I did not want to "remember". It was the memory of a small boy lying on stretcher in a Hamlet in Viet Nam. This boy was also dying, and like "Hot Lips", there was nothing I could do about it. The unconscious mind does not seem to choose between bad and good memories. It just indiscriminately flashes them. I suppose it is up to the conscious portion to determine the relative merits of each and to label them as good or bad, relevant or irrelevant.

How should I answer my son's question? Should she tell the guy he was dying? Should she not? I can see how a person could argue either point.

I decided that since I couldn't answer his question, I would simply tell him the story my memory had unfortunately dredged up.

The boy I told him about was involved in an incident that occurred a couple of months before l returned to the States, and the result of that incident has always stood out in my mind as one of the saddest moments of my life. For a couple of reasons this incident affected me even more than the loss of Doc.

l was not at the scene when Doc was injured. I did not see the pain in his face, and certainly was not able to speak to him. Doc was an adult who chose to be where he was. This incident involved a small child who had no choice.

l was with Gem in Phu Tan pretending to buy ice from one of the local villagers, when in actuality l was personally talking to an informant. It was not common and not very wise, but I was in a hurry and needed specific information that I had to personally ask and pay for.

A small boy ran by and when he saw me he tried to hide something that he was carrying. I immediately raised my M-16 and watched him very carefully to make sure that I was not a target of some kind, and then, as he got further away, I lowered my 16 and started to turn back

150

to what I had been doing. Then I realized what he had been carrying. It was a small canister, probably a white phosphorous grenade (called a Willie Peter). He had undoubtedly stolen it and was on his way to trade it on the black market for something much more valuable to him, food.

Unfortunately many small children stole booby-trapped grenades. They would sneak into the outer protective perimeters of American or Korean compounds, slip the trip wires off the grenades, stick in make-shift pins, and try to get back out of the concertina wire entanglements. Obviously this had to be done at night and if the guards on duty did not spot and shoot them as VC, they had an excellent chance of getting blown away by the booby-trapped grenades they were trying to steal.

We put out all kinds of propaganda trying to prevent these danger-ous theft attempts, but many of these children were hungry and the grenades were worth a lot of money on the black market.

Anyway, this boy had one and was running through the village with it. I turned back and saw him swerve to avoid a bucket of water being thrown out into the street by an old woman, and in the process of doing so he stumbled and dropped the grenade. As he scrambled to his feet the grenade went off. I don't know if he had failed to put a pin back in when he stole it, or if his makeshift pin had come out. Whatever the reason, he paid a terrible price for his mistake.

Phosphorous burns at an incredible temperature and a nearby hut burst into flames. The boy, by some fluke accident, was not instantly killed. I grabbed the radio from Gem and called our radio shack. I told Barnes, the corporal who was on radio duty, to run to Be, tell him what had happened, and to ask Be if he could get a medevac chopper for the boy.

This may seem a little strange in that I asked the Vietnamese village chief to call for an American medevac. All I can tell you is that if I had told Barnes to get hold of the major and have him call for the medevac, nothing would have happened. First, the major would not have made the call because it was not protocol. Second, the helicopter would not have been sent even if he had called because American helicopters were not sent for, nor did they transport wounded Vietnamese.

However, Be had so much pull in Tuy Hoa, I suppose because of his success in the district, that he could often get the Army and Air Force to do things outside of regular channels.

The boy was placed on an outside table, the fire in the hut was put out, and then there was really nothing for any of us to do but wait. I walked over to him and to my surprise he was conscious and could talk. He was burned so badly that he was in very little pain. His right hand was gone, his chest was horribly burned, and smoke came out of his mouth when he talked. Yet, he was very brave about it. He told me, through Gem, that his family needed the money for food and that his father had been instructing him as to how to get the grenades. He kept saying, "No VC". Evidently, even in his condition, his worst fear was that I would think he was a VC. Again, it was obvious to me that the boy was going to die. The smoke coming out of his mouth was an indication that he had inhaled a bunch of the phosphorous and of how badly he was burned inside.

After exchanging small talk with him for a few minutes I found that his hero was Dai Uy Be. He seemed to know all about the man, but had never met him.

I asked if he would like to meet Be and he gave me a pathetic smile as an answer. I used the radio again to call our compound. I told Barnes in no uncertain terms that he was to go get Dal Uy Be to come to our radio, and not to take no for an answer. Be's astonished voice came over the radio speaker a few minutes later and after my brief explanation he agreed to come right down.

He was there within five minutes with his usual flak jacket and an entire squad of bodyguards. He talked with the boy until the chopper arrived and promised the kid a job in the compound when he got well.

The chopper took the boy away. Be got back into his jeep, looked at me and shook his head. We both knew the boy had no chance.

The key words are, No Chance.

Normally I will fight tooth and nail with anyone who says we are a product of our environment. I simply do not believe that to be true. I cannot stand people who hide behind that statement, and who use it to explain why they are failures, or why they act a certain way. All individuals are continually faced with choices and the choices we make determine our destiny. The choices we make determine what chance we have to "make it" in the world. In America we all have a chance. We are all free to choose which path we follow. To me, it does not matter whether your parents were rich or poor, whether they were educated or illiterate, whether they were divorced or happily married, whether you were raised in a city, on a farm, in the mountains, or in the desert, here, you still have the chance to choose correctly.

This boy did not have that chance. His choices were being made for him while he was young and he was not going to live long enough to change that fact.

By the time I got back to the compound the pilot had already radioed back that the boy was dead.

That was it, probably a total of an hour out of my life. Nothing! Insignificant! Yet?

He had been such a nice, intelligent, brave kid. I had trouble accepting the fact that he was dead, while an hour earlier I had not even known that he existed. It was as if a close relation had just been uselessly killed. His entire life span, as far as I was concerned, had lasted only those few moments. And, in those few moments of talking with him, I had found him, liked him, and lost him.

I had seen many, many people killed while I had been in Nam, and a lot of those had been women and children. I thought I had become somewhat inured to death, but I was wrong. This useless, senseless, unnecessary death really bothered me. I had never found drinking to be a help in dealing with pain, and crying certainly didn't help, so I just went into my cubicle and thought, and prayed.

Chapter 18
DAI UY BE

A tour of duty in Viet Nam, lasted one year, and my year was to be over on June 15th. However, on March 30th I was sitting in Be's office having tea and talking about his hero, Douglas McArthur. Be had a huge picture of the General hanging behind his desk and was always willing to expound on the military tactics of the man. Be was of the opinion that, militarily, McArthur was the greatest general who ever lived. He liked to compare McArthur's military decisions with those of Napoleon, Caesar, and even the great southern general, P.T. Beauregard. Be's knowledge of history was truly unique. I had studied a considerable portion of military history and tactics, so we had some lively discussions.

Sgt. Clack knocked at the doorway and said that l had a radio call from Tuy Hoa. I took another sip of tea and told Be we would finish the debate at another time.

Mr. Clarkson was on the horn and said that he had some bad news for me. He said the Red Cross had just notified him that my mother was gravely ill and my presence was requested at home. My mother had had stomach troubles for years and it did not really surprise me to get the message, although I was naturally upset. The Red Cross is not allowed to make these requests unless the medical emergency has been checked out and it has to be very, very serious for the Army to acknowledge it, and allow a soldier to leave. I quickly packed up my belongings, said my good-byes and started out of the compound to catch the chopper that had landed on our pad and was waiting for me.

Be came out of his office and walked me out of the compound. He seemed very troubled and very apologetic. I think our previous conversation was still on his mind because he talked very carefully, as if it were a historic conversation that might be written down. I hate good-byes and usually try to get away from them as quickly as possible, but Be wanted to talk. I realize now that he was being very philosophical and even, as it turned out, prophetic.

He said, in his crisp but broken English that war was often more cruel to the innocent than it was to the guilty; adding that those who stayed at home often suffered more than those who left to fight. Then he said something that I will never forget, because although I came back to Viet Nam a month later, Be never spoke to me again.

His English was not perfect and I am clarifying it for you, but basically what he said was, "You do not like many of the things 1 do, and maybe someday I will be punished for them, but Americans do not understand the real pain of Viet Nam. I know you came here to try to help me and my people, and I thank you for that, but you do not understand. You cannot understand because you are not Vietnamese."

We shook hands for a long time. I looked him straight in the eyes and told him that he was right on all counts: I was trying to help, I did not like many things that he did, and I certainly could not think and feel like a Vietnamese.

"However, Dai Uy" I said, "I truly believe that you think what you are doing and the way you are doing things is right. I believe you care for your country, and for your people, and that you are risking your life every day to help both of them. I have never met a man in my life, and I doubt that I will ever meet many, who will love their country and their countrymen like you do yours."

Our right hands released, I turned and walked to the chopper.

Later, I found that he was right on one more thing, he was punished for his actions, but that story will come later.

By the time I got to Saigon with all my papers, it was March 31st. I sat around the Air Force base lounge waiting for a "hop" that would take me to California. At 11:30 p.m. a desk sergeant called me up, stamped my papers, and sent me out a gate to catch an Air Force transport. I had the old rifle that Doc had given me, but they stopped me at the gate and asked for my papers for it. I had what I had been given in Tuy Hoa and handed them over. The sergeant looked at them and told me that I would have to get them stamped by someone here in Saigon.

"OK," I replied, barely controlling my temper. "Who do I get to sign them, and where is the office?"

"Right around the corner, but no one will be there until 8:00am and your flight is leaving right now," he smiled as he said this.

He knew, since I was on emergency leave that I probably wouldn't wait around for another eight hours to get the dumb paperwork stamped, and then have to wait for another hop to the states. The guy was obviously planning on getting the rifle for himself.

Well, he was right as there was no way I was going to wait with my mother in critical condition. I shoved the rifle into his chest and walked out to the plane. Oh, what a mistake that was - not the shoving it into this chest – the not waiting those eight hours. It was to cost me dearly.

It wasn't the beautiful Braniff with the great looking stewardesses that I had when I flew over. In fact it was not a passenger plane at all. They put me in a C130, an Air Force cargo plane. I was placed in the back with the cargo in a sling seat suspended from the wall. My view was tons of crates wrapped in tarps. These crates were barely three feet in front of me. But, even the sling seats didn't bother me because I was going home. I had been given a 30 day Emergency Leave and was due to be back in Viet Nam on May 1st.

I landed in Oakland, took a commercial airline to Fresno, and was picked up by my wife. I spent one day with her, then flew to Tulsa, Oklahoma to see my mother.

Mom was indeed very ill, but instead of telling me of her immediate demise, the doctors had become optimistic about her chances. In fact, after I had been there for a few days, they were talking of sending her home.

She was a very religious woman and although she knew God's will would be done, she worried terribly about my being in Nam. The simple fact that I was home and safe probably did as much good as the doctors' medicines.

On the day they released her to go home, she insisted that she was well and that I should go back to my wife in California so that I could spend as much time with her as possible before I had to go back to Nam. I said my final good-bye to her and flew back to Joeline.

I spent the next two weeks enjoying the states and my wife. I talked to Mom every day on the phone and she seemed fully recovered from whatever it was she had. No doctor was ever able to explain what it was.

Near the end of the 30 days Joeline and I drove to the old Fort Ord Army base in Monterey to pick up my papers and check to see if the Army really wanted to go to all the trouble and expense of sending me all the way back when I only had about a month and a half left to serve. (Hey, it did no harm to ask, right?)

I figured the meeting would only take a minute or two because I assumed the guy at the desk would just laugh, hand me my papers, and tell when I was to catch the plane back to Nam.

Joeline sat in the shade of a beautiful tree overlooking the ocean and I suppose tried to forget the reason for our being there, while I tried to find the correct administrative office. The view she had was amazing. Fort Ord is on a hill and it has an unobstructed view of the Pacific. The only thing between her and the ocean was a few twisted, bent and scarred old cypress trees and some Torrey pines. That view could help anyone forget their worries and cares, at least for a little while.

I finally found an Army Colonel who could answer my question. Sure enough, there was a regulation that dealt with my specific situation. The regulation stated that if the individual in question had 45 days or less left to serve in Nam, then that individual was not to be sent back. Very clear!

He checked my papers, then rechecked them. 1 had exactly 46 days left in Viet Nam. I am not joking, it was nothing to joke about.

There was nothing to be done, Army regulations are exact and are obeyed to the letter - even to the day. If I had not left Saigon on that 11:30pm transport on the 31st, but had waited to get the paperwork on the rifle and left on the 1st, then I would have the rifle and would not be going back to Viet Nam. I would have spent the next 45 days safe and secure, probably manning a typewriter for someone at Fort Ord.

Not even a full day. My papers were clearly stamped that I had boarded my plane to leave Viet Nam at 23:30pm, if I had waited thirty minutes, then I would have had only 45 days left to serve there and I would not be going back. But, I didn't. I had 46 days.

So, two days later, I again said my good-byes to a tearful wife. It had to have been terrible for her. How many times was she going to have to go through this? As I said, I hate good-byes, but as Dai Uy had said, they are much harder on those being left behind.

Consider this. When I left for jungle school in Panama we said our good-byes because we thought I would go straight to Nam from there. We were at the airport and there were many other soldiers present who were going through the same thing. To this day Joeline starts crying every time she sees a soldier in an airport. It truly left a hidden scar that she will always carry.

Anyway, as it turned out I was flown to Charleston, S.C., for a few days of indoctrination, then back to California, where l was given a three day leave before I was sent on to jungle school. That gave us a few more days together, which we were grateful for, but it obviously resulted in another good-bye.

Then I left for Panama, knowing that I would be flying straight to Viet Nam after I completed jungle school.

But no, because after jungle school I was flown back to the states and given another three day leave. Yes, it was three more days we could spend together, but the good-byes were wearing on both our nerves.

After seven months in Nam I was given the six day Rest and Recuperation in Hawaii. After that we had to say good-bye again.

Remember that on each of these occasions we thought that I was going into the war zone and did not know if we would ever see each other again.

When I boarded the plane this time for Nam, I knew it would be the last time, so that helped a lot. However, I was headed into what would be the most dreadful 46 days of my life. (Although as things turned out, it was less than 46 days.)

When I arrived in Tuy An, the place was in an uproar. Major Lee, who had been the ranking US officer in the compound, had been transferred with no warning whatsoever. I was told that two Colonels had arrived by helicopter one day and they told him to pack, and to pack quickly. They waited and twenty minutes later, with him in tow, left the compound with no explanation to anyone. He had been gone for three days when I arrived and I found that Dai Uy Be was preparing to leave as well. He was also being transferred.

The fact that the major was transferred was no big deal, although the manner in which it was done was certainly unusual. However, Dai Uy Be leaving Tuy An District was nothing short of monumental. It was so unprecedented, and so unexpected that everyone was basically stunned into silence.

None of the Americans in the compound knew what was going on, but they had been told to stay away from all the Vietnamese in the compound and in the District. I obviously could not obey such an order since my entire operation in the DIOCC depended on my working with the Vietnamese. We were in Viet Nam for goodness sake, how could I stay away from the Vietnamese?

I tried to set up a meeting with Be, but was told he could not see me. So, I called a meeting of all the people in the DIOCC. Only then did I find out what had happened and what was going on.

I started the meeting with a very simple question. "What the hell is going on?"

Everyone talked among themselves for a moment, then Gem gave me this interpretation.

> A prisoner had been brought into the compound and was interrogated by Be. For some unknown reason, Major Lee was allowed in on the questioning. The prisoner was very uncooperative and answered every question with the same statement, "Long live Ho Chi Minh!"

160

Finally Be lost control. That slender thread of restraint that kept him seemingly sane most of the time, snapped. He became the cold, methodical, lethal killer I had seen a few times before. I was not there on this occasion, but I know the look that must have come into his eyes.

He grabbed the man's hair and pulled him up and out of the bunker. (Prisoners were always tied with their hands and feet pulled up behind them.) Once outside, Be began yelling orders. The prisoner was dragged out of the compound and thrown down on the same cement landing pad I had left from a month earlier.

From what I could find out, Major Lee simply stood watching the scene unfold in fascinated silence. He did nothing to try to stop what was happening and he did not aid or hinder its climax. His inability to react probably cost him his entire military career.

A soldier ran out of the ammo bunker with ten sticks of dynamite and quickly wrapped them together with tape. Then, the entire wad was taped to the prisoner's chest. A long, slow burning fuse was attached to the charge and Be lit it. Then he walked back to the prisoner and began asking him more questions. The man looked at the burning fuse for a few seconds and then began screaming at the top of his lungs, "Long live Ho Chi Minh!"

Dai Uy Be walked back into the compound and the prisoner was blown out of existence.

After the man was gone, Major Lee shook himself out of his trance and decided that this was not proper military procedure. He reported the incident to his superiors in Tuy Hoa and recommended that Be be punished. According to Barnes, the Major also insisted that he had tried to stop Be. The report was forwarded through US channels to Saigon where, evidently a visiting Senator got wind of it. He saw a chance to get a little publicity for himself, went to Be's superiors and threw a fit. Once the winds of dissent started blowing, they could not be stopped until someone had taken the blame.

Be's superiors were forced to send him out of the District as a "punishment". I understand that in actuality he was given a bigger and much more lucrative post near Saigon, but I never received any verification of this.

The Major had to be shipped out of Tuy An before the local Vietnamese found out that he was the one responsible for Be's being moved. They would have undoubtedly killed him if he had stayed in the District for only a couple of days once the news was out.

Hung said he would have shot him if he had known, and Hung did not make idle threats.

Dai Uy Be left the District a day after I arrived. He was given a departing hero's farewell with everyone cheering and waving to him. A lot of tears were shed over his departure. No American was allowed to go near him or the procession that saw him off. We were all ordered to stay in our building.

I desperately wanted to talk to him again, but it was simply not possible.

So, I was left in Tuy An with no District Chief, an angry populace, and a newly revitalized Viet Cong element. The VC no longer had a Dai Uy Be to fear and started to take advantage of the void immediately.

We fought off more attacks, had more soldiers and civilians killed and wounded, and had more bridges blown during the next month than in all of my previous ten months combined.

Be was a ruthless ruler, there is no doubt of that. He controlled the District with a firm, fearsome grip, but, he did control it. With him gone, there were no more safe areas in Tuy An. Hung advised me to stay out of the local hamlets unless he was with me. The VC were getting more powerful every day and now the South Vietnamese in the area, who once treated the Americans with respect even if it was often distant and detached, now seemingly hated us.

I was a short timer, with a little over a month to go, so I decided to lay low and ride out the rest of my tour as unobtrusively as possible. I knew that a new District Chief would eventually be assigned and I hoped that he would restore order, but it would take a few months and l would not be around to see the results.

Although l could probably avoid most of the military operations for a while, I could not avoid the moral and ethical nature of the entire situation. By all of our religious and American beliefs, the Major was absolutely correct in his actions, although he should have tried to stop it entirely.

But, look at the results. The prisoner was not saved, the district fell apart, hundreds of soldiers and civilians were killed or wounded due to the increased VC activity, a competent - if ruthless - District Chief was transferred, and the military career of an American major was probably ruined.

Be told me that he knew the Americans in Viet Nam were trying to help, but that we did not understand the ways of his people. He was definitely right. Our entire military operation in South East Asia was based on erroneous military and moral principles, based on past experience gained in totally different wars, and under considerably different circumstances and conditions.

Be was not punished or condemned by his people. He was only transferred because a few American big shots in Saigon threatened a few Vietnamese big shots. Be had to be transferred as an apparent punishment to appease the Americans. But, he probably was in fact given a promotion after the Americans had turned their backs and lost interest in the situation since there was no further political leverage to be gained.

One of our problems as Americans is that we believe ours is the one and only solution to a problem. We have difficulty seeing and understanding the other man's point of view.

In our past wars the other man's view was inconsequential. We simply sailed over, around, or thru him and his beliefs to get to the enemy. Then we blew the enemy away with superior firepower, tenacity, and advanced military tactics.

In Viet Nam, the superior firepower was ours, but it was useless against an enemy who applied our own Revolutionary War tactics against us. The firepower would have paid off if we had attacked the home of the North Vietnamese, Hanoi. But, our misguided ethics again got in the way. Our leaders wanted us to win the war, but they wanted us to win it without soiling our reputation. We could kill thousands of innocent people in South Vietnam, but we could not fight the real enemy in North Vietnam. We could bomb them a little, but we could not attack them in their backyard. Make sense?

Our tenacity was not there. How could it be with the Jane Fonda's of the world marching and calling us names? Those of us who were sent to Nam were trying to be good Americans, as our forefathers had been, and do what our country told us to do. We didn't want to be there, but our country sent us to fight, so we did our best under the circumstances. But we could not fight with certainty of purpose and tenacity, because our country was not certain.

Every newscast told of marches and riots protesting our being in Nam. They called us butchers and killers. Did they call the Marines on Iwo Jima killers?

Our country did not know what it wanted, so our movements were hindered while the enemies were strengthened.

As for our military tactics, they were absurd. The greatest nation in the world was outmaneuvered, psychologically, politically, and militarily by an enemy, the large majority of whom could not read nor write.

Please understand that I am not supporting Be's action. Had I been there, there would have been plenty of time for me to act, and I know I would have tried to stop him. This was a long drawn out affair, not like the instant killing of the prisoner in the first chapter where I had no chance to stop it. I really think that Be would have secretly welcomed by interference. I am sure he would have listened to me. His temporary insanity usually only lasted for a few seconds, a minute at the most. During this incident, I'm sure he had come back to reality by the time the fuse was lit, but since no one said anything, he simply could not back down on his own. He was probably waiting for the Major to object so that he would have had a reason to stop. As it was, Be just let the act play out to its horrible conclusion. I really feel that my not being there cost the lives of dozens of individuals, many of them children, and I will explain why I feel that way as we go along.

Be was wrong. In our moral judgment, as Americans, killing some-one in cold blood is never justified, even in a war. But, although I believe with all my heart that he was wrong by our standards, we were not in America. We were in Vietnam. His standards, his country's standards, their beliefs concerning right and wrong are different from ours. I am not saying that in any way he was right, and I think that before the dy-namite ignited, he knew he was wrong. But, he was trying to protect his country from the VC and North Vietnamese who were trying to, and eventually did, take over his country.

What he failed to realize, and what I'm sure I could have quickly made him understand, was that by letting the fuse burn to the end, he was behaving as badly as, or worse than the people from whom he was trying to protect his people.

Chapter 19
OFF DUTY HOURS

It has been said that war is long days of absolute, total boredom, interspersed with moments of extreme terror. That definition fits my life in the compound perfectly.

I would spend days pouring tediously over informant reports, correlating present information with past reports, and then filing them all away for future reference. The next day I would start all over again with a new batch of reports. And there, constantly, day and night, lying just beneath the surface of the boredom was the homesickness, that empty feeling that no amount of activity, or letters from home could completely fill. I suppose that is the reason that, supposedly, so many of the American GI's in Viet Nam turned to drugs. However, in my entire year there I never saw or heard of one man, American, Vietnamese, or Korean, taking any - unless you count the beetle nuts the Vietnamese chewed.

Sorry, I hate to ruin your perception of a soldier's life in Viet Nam. I know it does not fit the movies you have seen or the horror stories you have heard about American GI's becoming drug addicts. Did it happen in some places in Viet Nam? I'm sure it did. But, I have talked to many of the other coordinators for the PHOENIX programs and none of them had much trouble with drugs in their areas of operation either.

In a way, it really makes me mad that there is this misconception. Soldiers in WWI, WWII, Korean, etc. had their problems also, but the general consensus about Viet Nam era soldiers is that we were all drug addicts or alcoholics. Nothing could be further from the truth. To stay alive in the jungles of Viet Nam you needed to have all of your senses working at maximum efficiency. If you were some marijuana hop head and went staggering around in a haze you would not have lasted a day in my area of operation. If you wanted to find drug addicts in the late 60's and early 70's, all you had to do was look it the lines of protesters in the U.S. They were there where they were safe, they were not trying to stay alive in Viet Nam.

Anyway, I will get off my soapbox and get back to the story.

On nights when 1 would accompany the PRU out on ambushes, 1 would spend long hours crouching uncomfortably on the wet ground, with bugs crawling over me, and mosquitoes swarming around my head. On many of the nights we would see nothing, and wearily trudge back to the compound at dawn to get a few hours of sleep before I went back to the paperwork.

On other nights the boredom would be "relieved". Someone would open fire and for a few moments the tediousness and homesickness would be replaced by the purest terror possible. In those few moments, all other sensations were subdued and the overpowering will for survival took over.

Fire fights usually only lasted for a few seconds. After that, the enemy either withdrew or we did, depending on the situation and our location in the district. It was not a conventional war. There was not a "front" as in all past wars. The war was all around us and it was nowhere. One moment we would be surrounded by "friendlies", the next moment by the enemy, and the following moment by "friendlies" again.

And, what many do not realize is that, outside of all of this, life went on. At night in the compound, time did not stand still. We had hours and hours with nothing to do. We had to find diversions for the time not spent fighting or preparing to fight. 1 tried all kinds of things. I had my wife send me a basketball goal and ball. I nailed the goal on the outside wall of our building and we spent hundreds of off duty hours playing "horse".

Clack had a football and many of us played catch to pass the daylight non-duty hours.

Of course, as I said, night was the worst. If we were not on a mission, we had twelve hours to fill with something. If we just sat around and thought of home and felt sorry for ourselves we would go crazy.

Writing and reading letters was the favorite past time for the Viet Nam soldier, as it has been for every soldier since Revolutionary War days. But, you can only spend so much time doing that. There had to be something else with which to pass the leisure time.

To fill in the time not spent on letters, I had Joeline send us games. The first she sent, and the one that was probably the most ironic, was Risk. If you have never played it, it is a board game in which you try to take over the world by attacking other armies with your own. The idea of us sitting around in jungle fatigues with our M 16's by our side and playing this war game has always seemed comical to me. But, everyone loved it. The Major who was in the compound at that time wrote to his wife and asked her to buy one for his family. He wanted to be able to play it when he got home.

We tried Monopoly, but had to stop that one night after a Vietnamese stole all of the money. That's right, they stole our Monopoly money.

We had been playing in the dining area, and had been playing for a few nights in a row. I know we had been loud and rowdy. You know how guys get when they're playing a game and really getting into it. We were each yelling about the money like it was real and having a great time. I'm sure that if it had been real money we would not have been acting any differently. When I play a game I play to win and play money or real money, it makes no difference, I just want to win. The rest of the guys were the same way and when one of them got paid big on a property, you would have thought he had won the lottery.

On that night, when the game was over, I was on radio watch, so everyone went to bed and left the clean-up to me. I went to answer a radio call, and as I walked back to the table I saw a Vietnamese running out the back with the Monopoly money in his hands. We had played the game so energetically that he believed the money to be some new form of MPC. He must have gotten into a lot of trouble when he tried buying something on the black-market with it.

169

OK, MPC? That stands for Military Payment Currency. To try to cut down on black-marketing, the U.S. Government paid everyone there in MPC and not "greenbacks". It was paper money in different colors, and in fact it looked a lot like Monopoly money. Every few months, without notice, someone would show up in our compound and tell us that we had to exchange our old MPC for new MPC. After that day the old MPC was worthless. Therefore, anyone in the black-market who held MPC would suddenly find it worthless. In many places, it was called Monopoly money.

After the Monopoly money was gone, and we tired of Risk, we began to play Bridge. We played it for about a month, and then two of the foursome who could play, left and we couldn't teach any of the remaining members in the compound enough to make the game worthwhile. Besides, while the four of us were playing, everyone else in the compound had to find their own diversions, and since many couldn't find any on their own, we began to have discipline and drinking problems.

We turned to Poker and probably spent most evenings for three months trading money back and forth with that game. More could play it and it did not take the intelligence of Bridge, so it seemed to work out very well.

Of course, I could always go into Tuy Hoa. It was a fairly large city and when I went there, I stayed at the Air Force Base. They had flushing toilets and ice cream. I know the two do not go together, but I remember that I looked forward to both. The ice cream was certainly not like the Italian Gelato we get in Guatemala, and didn't compare to any Tom and Jerry flavor, but believe me when I was lying out in the hot, tropical jungle on an ambush, the very thought of it nearly drove me crazy. Once, I even went into a sort of movie theater they had there. The John Wayne movie, Green Berets was showing. Now, I am a huge John Wayne fan and consider him, like most people do, a true American Hero. However, I have never heard so much laughter in my life as there was in that theater during that movie. The movie was definitely a Hollywood version of Viet Nam. Ironically, I was in Fort Benning, Georgia when the movie was being filmed there.

On one of my trips to Tuy Hoa I found that there was a Special Services office there and that I could get a projector and movies from them. The movies were old and some in poor shape, but I found they were a big hit with the Vietnamese, most of whom couldn't understand any of the words. I would set the projector up in the middle of the compound when I had a movie and word would spread. So many showed up for the movies that I often wondered who was guarding us.

The Vietnamese especially liked slap-stick comedy and westerns. I suppose the dialogue in those two kinds of movies was so unimportant that they could follow what was being said without knowing the language.

One night as we were watching a John Wayne western, the new District Chief received a call that a bomb had gone off in Phu Tan and that the town was under attack. Everyone quickly dispersed.

I went to the mortar pit and took inventory to make sure everything was ready in case it was needed. Within a few moments the District Chief called the Major over and told him that there had been no attack and no bomb. Someone had thrown a grenade into a house in Phu Tan and that was it. He wanted it checked out and asked if I would see about bringing the wounded back to the compound and finding a way to get them to a hospital if necessary.

Since Doc was gone, I took the new corpsman, the new radio-man, and accompanied the District Chief's guards out of the compound and down to the hamlet. I realized that the entire thing could be a hoax to get some of us out of the compound, and if it was, then I was driving into a trap. My PRU's were out on ambushes, so I did not even have them for protection.

Since Dai Uy Be's departure, the Viet Cong in the area had increased their activity and we were constantly getting people shot. I was even more apprehensive because I had been getting informant reports indicating a large enemy build up in the district.

We reached Phu Tan and found the house where the grenade had gone off. One man had been killed, but there were no wounded. I had a very uneasy feeling about the whole matter. I found that the man had three children and yet all of them and the wife had come out without a scratch. There seemed nothing more that I could do, so I got my group together and headed back to the compound.

We started to leave the hamlet and then all of a sudden I stopped the jeep. The guards in the jeeps behind me came up to find out what was wrong. I couldn't tell them. I just knew that something was not as it should be. My senses were on edge and I could not explain why. I sent two men up the road and told them to look carefully for any signs of mines. I thought maybe the VC had placed a mine to catch us on our way back. They didn't find anything so we slowly drove back to the compound and nothing happened.

I received a few snickers from some of the Vietnamese for my pains, but that didn't bother me at all. I still felt something was strange about the entire incident.

We started the movie where we had left off and that should have been the end of the whole matter. The next day, however, I sent Gem to Phu Tan to snoop around. I told him to see if he could find out anything about the dead man.

A few hours later he came back and told me there was a rumor going around; yes even in Vietnamese villages there are rumors. It seems that the dead man's wife had been seen recently with another man and everyone felt she had thrown the grenade herself.

In Viet Nam there was no crime. If something was stolen, the VC did it. If someone was killed, the VC were responsible. The woman had taken the opportunity to get rid of her husband and as far as anyone knew, the VC did it. I felt better. My senses had not been wrong. As for the woman? A few weeks later she married the other man.

The next day I returned to my paperwork. Not only had the VC activity in the area increased since Be's departure, but my informant reports had become less and less valid. That afternoon I called in the Vietnamese intelligence people in the DIOCC, along with Hung, and Gem. I went over a few of the reports and then threw them in the trash. In no uncertain terms I told all of the intelligence people that if the information did not get more accurate, then all money would be cut off. They did not take the news in the best of humor and were grumbling when I dismissed them. I watched them for a minute and saw that several of them went straight to the District Chief's office.

Then I turned to Hung and Gem and told them that I wanted them to start taking action into their own hands with these people, these informants, who were feeding us incorrect reports.

"They are protecting the VC, Hung. Are you going to let them get away with that?" Then I took another step which I know Hung did not expect.

"And, I am not certain, but I am getting the impression that our own Vietnamese intelligence people in the DIOCC are not helping us much. In fact, I am pretty sure that some of them are writing up these phony reports themselves."

I asked them if they had anything to say. I could tell that they did.

Hung went first. He said that the Vietnamese of the district were very unhappy with the Americans because of what had happened with Be. The word had got out that the Colonel had "turned" Be in and thus, it was very hard to get any information or cooperation from the people in the district.

"I'm not denying anything that went on, Hung. I was not here, so I simply can't be sure. I have heard the rumors just like you have. So, let's assume they are true, are we just going to let the VC take over because of something a stupid Colonel did. I hate the VC just as much as you do Hung and I am sick of them injuring and killing children. I am going to do something about it and I will have a much better chance if I have your help. Are you going to help me or are you going to sit around and pout about what happened to Dai Uy? He was my friend too. You know that Hung!"

After Gem translated, he and Hung stared at me for a moment. I had never talked that way to Hung, but I was past caring about formalities. I was mad and I needed Hung's help.

They didn't walk out, so I took that as a good sign. I calmed down and asked if they had any suggestions about what we could do with the villagers to get them back on our side.

He sadly shook his head that he didn't. He just said that no one was blaming me, but that I should still be very careful in the district, and probably not go out of the compound anymore without him.

Great, now I had to watch for Viet Cong and the local Vietnamese as well. Could things get any worse? I found out a few seconds later that they could.

Gem started talking and told me what had been bothering him, along with all this other crap. He had just been drafted into the Regular Army and would not be able to be my interpreter much longer.

When I asked if that was what he wanted he said, "No". He would rather stay with me, but since Be was gone, no one had any power to do anything about it.

I assured him that I would talk to the District Chief and that I would take care of it.

And, speaking of the District Chief, he picked that exact moment to come into my office. Hung and Gem quickly and quietly left. The DC was very upset and asked why I was not going to give his men in the DIOCC any more money.

I was surprised by his aggressive attitude and then I suddenly realized that he must have been getting a cut of their pay since his arrival. He didn't care about my informants or the Vietnamese in my DIOCC, he cared about his losing money.

Honestly it was all I could do to keep from tearing the guy apart. Instead, I kept my composure and calmly explained about the informant reports; that I felt we were simply getting made up reports with no validity whatsoever. For his benefit I said, "I am paying these guys a lot of money and they are just lying to me. I will not stand for it and if I have to I will get hold of people I know personally in Saigon and tell them to simply close this DIOCC because the people here are taking CIA money and have stopped doing the job they are getting paid to do."

He backed down immediately and said he was sure I was mistaken, but that he would look into it. Then he asked me to please continue to see that the men were paid until then.

I looked him right in the eyes and said that I would think about it. Then I told him about Gem being "drafted into the Army". I asked him if there was something he could do to stop that from happening.

He stared right back at me and said that he would think about it. Then he gave me a smirk and left.

I was being blackmailed and I did not like it. Things seemed to be falling apart and I just got madder and madder the more I thought about it. I had less than a month left in country and although I definitely had a short-timer's attitude, I was not about to quit. I wanted to fight back.

An hour later we received a call that a hamlet in the district was under heavy attack. The District Chief said that this time it seemed to be for real. I called Tuy Hoa and asked for a couple of gun-ships and transport helicopters.

By the time we got an RF company together, aboard the choppers and to the site, the fire fight was over and there didn't seem to be much else to do.

Evidently the local soldiers in the hamlet had started a volleyball game and had their weapons leaning up against the buildings. A squad of VC sneaked into the hamlet, got between the local forces and their weapons and opened fire. The local hamlet guards had to run for their lives; nine of them didn't make it.

Nine RF soldiers dead, twenty of our weapons captured, and not one enemy even wounded. Not even a shot fired at the enemy. Had Be been in the District, this would never have happened.

When the District Chief returned, I went to him and told him that this was the same sort of behavior as the misleading reports and that he had better get his district together. I did not wait for him to try to form a rebuttal in English and just left his office.

I returned to our building and tried to call Mr. Clarkson on the radio. Something had to be done and I was hoping he could help me put some pressure on this District Chief before we were all wiped out. Instead, I got even worse news. Clarkson was being transferred to Australia. Australia, what in the world was a man with his qualifications going to do in Australia?

175

This really surprised me because I had talked to him the week before and he had been looking forward to being transferred back to the states when his tour was up here in three months.

He told me he had been away from his family for too long and was now owed a stateside job. The guy I talked to gave out way more information than he should have, but he knew me and knew that Clarkson and I were tight. He said the guy who called had given Clarkson an ultimatum - he could take the Australian job or quit. I never talked to Clarkson again, so I don't know which he chose. I'm not even sure if he worked directly for the CIA or for some other clandestine organization.

Things were not working out for anyone and I seemed to be in the middle of it all. A couple of months ago, the U.S presence had finally seemed to be taking a toll on the VC. The Tet offensive had been a decisive defeat for them, regardless of what the American public thought, and we had been nearing a total victory in our own District. Now, things had suddenly turned sour. I had never seen it worse.

I had a little over three weeks left, but if things did not turn around soon, it was going to be very difficult to make it through those three weeks unless I simply sat in the compound and did nothing.

Chapter 20
CHILDREN

We had arrived at our ambush positions an hour earlier and a long, wet, miserable night lay ahead of us. The early monsoon rain had been coming down for a week and made a depressing war even more unbearable. Morale in the compound was extremely low and it had begun to affect my men and me.

After I returned from the emergency leave, the enemy actions had intensified, I had stopped getting accurate information, and the District had basically started blackmailing me. So, I decided to just end my tour by staying in the relative safety of the compound. At first I had been very mad and was determined to fight back, but then I just said to heck with it. It is their war, if that is how they want to play it, then I will just serve my last few weeks and then leave. I did so for a few days, but nothing was getting done, and I started to feel guilty about just sitting around in the compound and shuffling papers.

I decided that with or without Hung's help I had to get back outside. I planned a series of ambushes based on some old informant report, but I kept putting off the ambush. I told myself that I would wait so that the rain might eventually let up. But, that was just an excuse and I knew it, and it was not even a very good one. The real reason was that I had begun to be afraid. I only had a little time left in country and had suddenly become very "conservative". Finally, I got my act together, and called Hung to the DIOCC and told him to get his men together - we were going out.

He gave me one of his strange looks, and then smiled wildly. He was ready. He too had obviously decided that no matter what else had happened he wanted to go after VC. I don't know how long he would have waited before he came to talk to me or until he took matters into his own hands. Regardless of what had happened with the Colonel, he knew that he and I made a good team.

I can't tell you how relieved I was to learn that he was still on my side. I had decided to go out anyway, but to go not knowing if the PRU were going to back me would have been insane. Now, with Hung back on my side, my mood brightened considerably.

The VC had been taking advantage of the low visibility offered by the downpour to increase their mining of Highway One and their booby trapping of many of the major trails in the District. In the last few days, five South Vietnamese RF soldiers had been killed and seven others had been wounded by different traps.

The ambush that I had arranged for this night, although officially set up to try to get a group of VCI's, was essentially aimed at trying to catch some of the VC who were laying the traps, and to try to deter others from laying more. Again, not specifically my job, but it had to be done and I had the best troops to accomplish the task.

Before leaving the compound, Hung, Gem, and I spent several hours going over a map of the District and my informant reports, trying to decide where the VC were coming from, which trails they were using, and trying to anticipate where they would lay their next batch of trip wired grenades, punji pits, and mines.

It was like trying to pin down the wind, but we had to attempt to stop them, or at least limit their movements.

Three hours after dark we had sneaked out of the compound by using a secret exit through the mine fields and concertina wire that I had forced Di Uy Be to set up for us months ago in case our compound was ever overrun. I had a hard time convincing him that it was needed, as he believed that we should fight to the last man if that ever happened. I remember that back then I sure felt better once we had a "back door." That fighting to the last man was certainly not in my plans.

We had never used this exit and I was extremely nervous of using it this time, but it was the only way to conceal our movements. Hung had learned, while I was on leave, that his and my movements were being carefully monitored by the VC. They had spies in the district and they were tracking all of our moves every time we left the compound.

After several hours of very careful, slow movement, Gem, another PRU named Bao, and I concealed ourselves very near Chi Duc Hamlet. I had nothing to eat all day, and the smell of the evening meals being prepared nearly drove me crazy as I crouched under a large tree and tried to forget how wet, cold, and depressed I really felt. The scene reminded me of one of those Christmas cards where a man on a horse in a snow storm approaches a snug looking little cabin, with smoke coming out of the chimney. The inscription below would read, "Home at Last", or "A Haven from the Storm", or something like that.

Unfortunately, I was in the position of being able to see the haven and smell the food, but was not able to go inside. I had to sit out in the storm for the entire night, for the purpose of killing anyone who walked down the trail. It was quite a contrast to the peaceful picture in my mind.

On occasions like this, I had long ago developed the ability to let part of my mind wander to happier, safer times and places, while another part of it concentrated on the dangers around me. I perfected this ability during the summer months of my high school years. During those summers, I used to haul horses across country for my father, and on these long trips by myself, I could drive for hundreds of miles with part of my mind on other things while a portion of it dealt with the problems of the road. Sometimes, I would arrive in a town and hardly remember any of the countryside I had driven through to get there. However, I remembered the poems I had composed during the trip. The ability to do this always helped to pass the time, but on this occasion the misery of the situation prevented me from truly "getting away".

As the long hours slowly passed, I got colder and wetter and more cramped and uncomfortable until finally I felt I couldn't stand it anymore. At 0200 hours I carefully stood up and stretched my legs. My fatigues were soaked underneath my poncho, my boots and socks were saturated and I was extremely cramped from the hours of alternately sitting, crouching, and kneeling on the wet ground.

The rain was coming down as hard as ever and it was difficult to see more than a few feet down the trail. Had I a choice, I would have called off the ambushes and gone into a hut for the remainder of the night. But, there was no way to call them off. To move around meant instant death, either at the hands of the VC, or more probably at the hands of my own men. The other PRU ambush positions could not see any better than I, and they would shoot anything that moved on the trail or in the jungle around them. We did not carry any radios for communication between the ambush sites, although I had a radio in case I needed to get hold of our compound for support.

I had no choice but to get through the night as well as I could. I kneeled back down and tried to put part of the misery and loneliness out of my mind.

We had no visitors the entire night and neither did any of the other ambushes. At dawn we rendezvoused at a prearranged site, Hung and 1 sent out point and flank men and we started the long walk back to the compound.

Five minutes later the radio man came up to me and said I had a call from the District Chief. The DC informed me that a few moments earlier he had received word that a group of children had activated a booby trap at a specific location and he wanted us to check it out.

I took out my map, changed our return route somewhat and headed for the coordinates I had been given. It took us a little over thirty minutes to get there and even that was too soon for me when I saw what awaited us.

In the early morning hours the children had been going out of their hamlet to round up their water buffalos for the day's work, when one of them tripped a mine. They were all walking in a group and I suppose laughing and talking as any children would be, so the resulting explosion did tremendous damage. Four of them were killed instantly and eight of the remaining twelve were wounded.

Death, pain, and cruelty are obvious consequences of war and I had become very callous to much of it. But, the injury and death of children still affected me very deeply. Who knows what one of these children could have become? Maybe one of them would have grown up and been able to change the living conditions of thousands of his countrymen. Now, these children didn't exist. And, what of their parents? Think of the suffering they were going through. It was just not right, or just, or fair. Yes, I know the old saying, but it is not true. War should still be fair. It should be fought, if it had to be fought, by adults. Children should be left alone.

The consequences of that explosion were gruesome and I refuse to dredge up the old memories or subject you to the details, so I will just deal in specifics. As I have already stated, four of the children were killed instantly, two more died before I arrived, and one died in the medevac that I had called to take them to the hospital in Tuy Hoa.

Seven children were dead. Of the other five who were wounded, three of them had lost, or would lose limbs and/or eyes. The reasons for their death and suffering are hard for me to understand. But, I can't understand the terrorist actions that are going on in our world today, so there's no reason to believe that I can explain and/or understand those of nearly 45 years ago.

I did as much as I could, which wasn't much. One of the PRU was a pretty good medic and I'm sure he saved a few of the children by his actions.

The medevac arrived, we loaded the wounded on board and continued our walk back to the compound. The villagers were left to deal with their grief and go on with their lives.

When we finally got back to the compound I found that the MACV team had an operation going on that day with a couple of the District Chief's companies. I wasn't up to trekking across anymore country, but I did want a chance to forget what I had just seen. I changed my socks and fatigues and agreed to ride on one of the choppers as a spotter.

The District Chief had been informed that a large VC force was supposed to be quartered at a certain location, (the coordinates of which I don't have in any of my notes), and he wanted to get them.

I rode around in one of the choppers for three hours. The total kill for that operation was five pigs and 2 water buffalos - VC of course.

That night a VC assassination team infiltrated into Chi Duc hamlet and killed two civilians - one of whom had been a Chu Hoa the year before. We had missed them by one night. My informant reports and our intuition had been correct, we had simply been in the right place one night too early. That's the way in worked in the war we were waging. We had to be at the right place at the right time and that was very difficult to do when there were only 20 of us and we were trying to cover an entire district.

I wanted very badly to get the VC who were setting up the traps. Their activity was causing me to take the war personally, and I kept telling myself that I couldn't do that   However, these people were crossing that thin line that separates war from atrocity and they were doing it in my district. They were targeting innocent, unprotected young children and I had to try to stop them.

When the Korean compound got hit with satchel charges the following night I figured that they were the same group I was after and decided to go see the Korean intelligence officer to determine whether we could work a little closer in trying to eliminate the culprits.

When I arrived at the ROK compound I found that the only damage was to one of their 105mm guns. No one had even been injured. I took their S-2 officer a bottle of whiskey and he took me to lunch. It was my first taste of Kimchee and l loved it. He liked the whiskey and drank enough so that he talked a little too much.

He told me, very confidentially of course, that the barrel of that 105 had been worn out for months but they couldn't get a replacement for it. Finally they blew up the gun themselves and blamed it on VC satchel charges. He had already received word that a new gun was on the way, and they would get it within a few days.

The incident added to my understanding of the Korean psyche, but got me no promise of any help in catching the VC that I was after. I was frustrated, angry, and had hoped I might get some commitment of help.

On the way back to the compound I received a radio call from the Major. He told me that a Vietnamese Lieutenant had just come in wounded. He and his buddy, another VN Lieutenant, were ambushed by the VC and he had been shot in the arm, but managed to run away and escape. His friend had been shot in the leg and couldn't get away. The District Chief was sending a platoon of soldiers to meet me and we were to sweep the area where the two men had been ambushed and try to locate the missing man.

I knew that we would probably not find him alive, but I held out hope that we would. I had seen enough death and it was wearing me down. I started imagining finding him hiding in some bushes and the joy that would be on his face when he saw us. Man, that would be a happy occasion and we all needed a lift.

We didn't get it, we found him, lying half in and half out of a ditch, with two bullet holes in his head. The VC were not to be found.

That same afternoon a group of children who were members of a group called a Junior RD (Redevelopment) Team, which was similar to our boy and girl scouts, were shot at while at a party. It may surprise you that there were scouts in Viet Nam, and even that there were parties, but remember, kids will be kids regardless of the circumstances or of their countries politics.

Anyway, three of them were killed. Why? I have no idea!

That was it. I had to stop this insanity. I called Hung in and told him to personally go to every informant on my payroll and tell them that there would be no more money for anything other than information on who these people were that were killing children. I told him I did not care what the District Chief thought or said. I controlled the money and I would not pay another dime for any information unless it was on these people. I told him he was free to use whatever means he needed to get me the information. Then, we were all going hunting. These people were going to pay, and I did not care where we had to go to get them.

All of this went against my orders. As a DIOCC advisor I was supposed to use my power to catch VCI, not ordinary terrorist squads. But I really didn't care. What was the Army going to do, fire me? I was going to use every bit of CIA money I could get my hands on, and every dime I had of my own, to get these butchers.

The money, or rather, the fact that I had cut off all money, started to bring results immediately. I realized that I should have got mad and done this sooner. During the following few days the information began to roll in. One small bit of information that kept appearing in the different reports was that the same squad was planning something against Tuy An Hamlet This was the nearest hamlet to our compound and generally considered a safe area for our forces and those on our side.

When I had accumulated enough "facts", I took the reports to the District Chief. He had received many of the same reports but did not believe the VC would do anything with so many of his forces near.

I decided to follow my own hunches and told Hung to get his men ready for an ambush the following night. My information again proved correct but, unfortunately, I was one night late in reacting to it.

That very night the VC entered Tuy An and set a large fire. In total, 138 homes were burned and seven people were killed - three of them were children.

The District Chief sent in his official report and said that the fire had been started by a woman making candy. He refused to admit that the VC were brave enough to act that overtly in a hamlet so close to his headquarters. It would look bad on his record.

As for the VC who had seemed so set on killing children, I could give you some glorious story about how we captured them and made them pay for their crimes. But, I can't do that. As I said earlier, if I had only been there when Be needed my assistance, he would have still been in the District and all of those children would probably still be alive. I wasn't, and it seemed that without him I was unable to stop the senseless killings.

Unfortunately, as so often happens in a war, this story did not end happily. Before I could "get them", I was again suddenly pulled out of the district. In fact I was pulled completely out of Viet Nam.

Chapter 21

HOME AT LAST

My final departure from Viet Nam was hurried and hectic. A few weeks before I was supposed to end my tour, the Army received another emergency call from the Red Cross concerning my mother. She was back in the hospital and her condition was listed as critical.

I again quickly packed my belongings and said my goodbyes. This time they were short and not at all painful.

Most of the people I had spent the year with had already moved on. The ones in the compound when I left were strangers to me. Be was gone; Gem had been drafted into the Regular Army; the MACV team had moved into a compound of their own; Major Kolb and Captain Wayne were back in the states; Major Lee had been transferred; Doc was at Walter Reed; my radio men, Barnes and Clack, were back with their families; and Hung was out on a two day operation with the PRU. Lt. Vick was the only one left whom I really knew and who really knew me.

I picked up my bags and boarded the waiting chopper. As it rose over the compound and aimed west, I felt something which was totally unexpected. I was actually a little sad to be leaving the district of Tuy An, and the country of Viet Nam. It is a beautiful country, and could be one of the finest tourist spots in the world. It has spacious, beautiful beaches; thick green jungles, and soaring cliffs. I knew that I would never be able to return and I was feeling regret at the fact that I would never be able to show my wife where I had spent such an important year of my life. But, most importantly, I felt that I was leaving a job undone. The VC who were killing children were still there. How many more innocent children would suffer the same fate? If I stayed a little longer, maybe I could help.

The District was not even as safe as it had been when I arrived. I had done nothing to stop the VC. They were more powerful now than they had been. I then understood why so many GI's "re-upped", and spent a second or third tour there. They wanted to finish something. I was feeling a great deal of regret, but I have told you many times, I am not a hero. Yes, I was feeling bad about leaving, but there was no way in the world that I ever considered signing up for another tour.

A month before, I had received a letter from the Army. Basically it said that if I would sign on the dotted line they would make me a Captain. I wrote them back and asked where my next tour of duty would be. Someone actually wrote back and said I could basically pick my station. Of course, after one year, I would be back in Viet Nam. I said, "No, Thank You".

Don't get me wrong. I liked the Army. I just could not see myself going on a hardship duty, having to leave my family, every other year. I have tremendous respect for those who have made a career in the military. Without them, we would not have the freedoms we enjoy. It just was not the life for me. Most Americans do not truly understand what these men and women do for us, what they sacrifice year after year so that the rest of us can remain safe at home. I do, and every member of every military branch has my utmost respect.

The different flights I had to take to get to Saigon were uneventful, and once I reached there, I was immediately put on a plane to the states. It touched down in Oakland, and I stepped back on American soil. There were no bands playing, no one throwing flowers or waving flags. There was in fact no one to welcome me home or thank me for fighting in a war for my country. One guy outside the gate tried to bum some money off of me and that was the extent of my welcome.

It took a full day for me to complete all of the Army's paperwork and end my life as a soldier in the United States Army.

The following day, in Visalia, California, I was reunited with my wife. Our joy was, however, short lived, because a few hours later we received a call from my father. He had called to tell me that my mother had died. She was a strong Christian woman and there is no doubt in my mind that her prayers, along with the prayers of others, protected me through many tight spots during that year in Viet Nam. I know that many times, during my long hours in those dark jungles, I kept repeating a verse she taught me when I was very young. "Yea, though I walk through the valley of death, I will fear no evil: for Thou art with me..."

She clung to life long enough to get the news that I had landed safely in Oakland. I like to think that she passed on at peace, knowing that her son was back on American soil and was no longer in a war. She certainly deserved that last bit of comfort.

We made flight arrangements and flew back to Van Buren, Arkansas, for the funeral.

Many years have passed since my tour of duty in Viet Nam. The country fell to Communism only a couple of years after I left and I have no idea what happened to the people who fought alongside of me. I think of Hung and Be often and wonder what happened to them. If they did not get out of the country before it fell, I fear that they did not make it at all.

Some say that we were wrong to go there, and that all of our fighting proved useless, but I disagree. A person, and a country, must choose the road which seems to head in the correct direction and then follow that road. No one can go back and undo the past. We don't get a second chance. I, and my country, tried to do the right thing, to make the right decisions, and to help another country in a time of great need.

The fact that a lot of my fellow countrymen did not agree and spent their time trying to destroy our government and country rather than fighting for it, is their problem, and not mine.

They have to live with their actions.

I am proud of the fact that my country tried to help. I disagree with some of its strategies and I know the war could have been won. But, I blame that loss on the protesters and some poor military decisions, and certainly not on the soldiers who fought there.

It's easy to sit back and say that, according to our U.S. moralistic viewpoint, Be and Hung were wrong in some of their actions and in their treatment of many problems.

They, however, were trying their very best to protect their country. How many of us have done, or would do as much, for our own? If Communism were taking over our government, if we were actually being invaded, would we have the will to fight for as long and as hard as they did?

I hope that we would, but even more fervently I pray to God that we never have to find out.

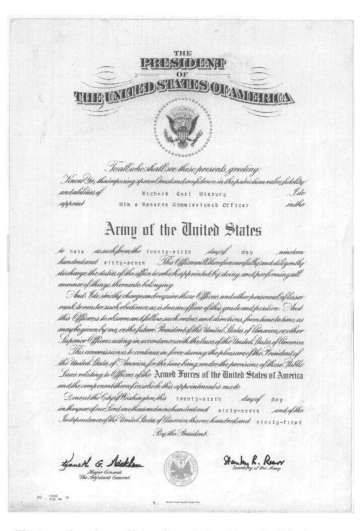

This is my Certificate of being Commissioned into the U.S. Army

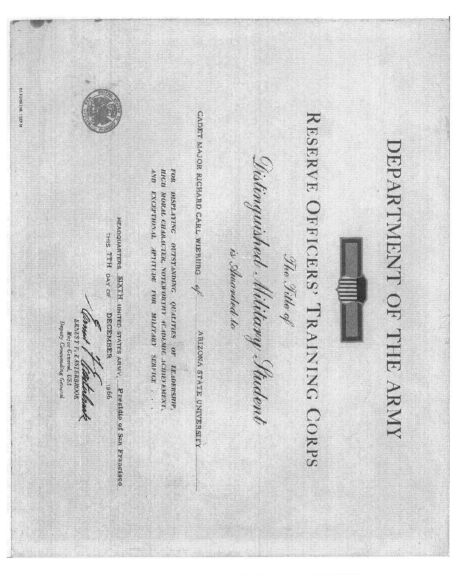

I was selected as a Distinguished Military Student by the ROTC Detachment at Arizona State University

190

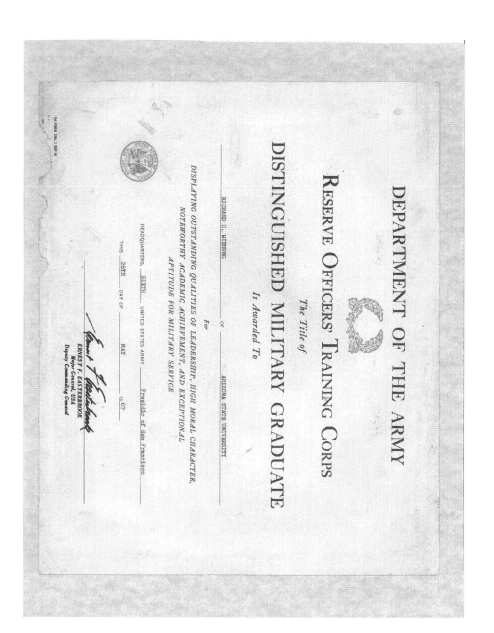

I was selected as a Distinguished Military Graduate by Arizona State Univ.

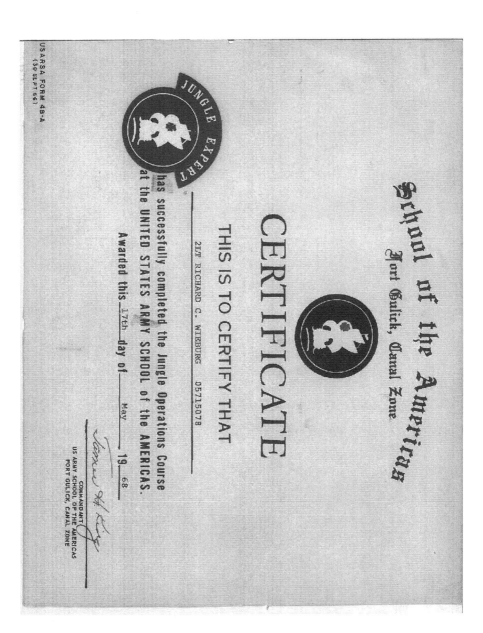

A Graduation Certification from Jungle School in Panama

I was awarded this by the South Vietnamese Government for my service to their country

CERTIFICATE OF RECOGNITION

RICHARD C. WIEBURG

In recognition of your service during the period of the Cold War (2 September 1945 - 26 December 1991) in promoting peace and stability for this Nation, the people of this Nation are forever grateful.

SECRETARY OF DEFENSE

This was given to me years after I returned to the states. The U.S. government finally decided to recognize VN era veterans.

Made in the USA
San Bernardino, CA
03 April 2014